# Rain Forests
## of the
# World

Volume 9
Reforestation–Spider

**MARSHALL CAVENDISH**
**NEW YORK • LONDON • TORONTO • SYDNEY**

Marshall Cavendish Corporation
99 White Plains Road
Tarrytown, New York
10591-9001

Website: www.marshallcavendish.com

Consulting Editors: Rolf E. Johnson, Nathan E. Kraucunas

Contributing Authors:    Theresa Greenaway, Jill Bailey, Michael Chinery, Malcolm Penny, Mike Linley, Philip Steele, Chris Oxlade, Ken Preston-Mafham, Rod Preston-Mafham, Clare Oliver, Don Birchfield

Discovery Books
    Managing Editor: Paul Humphrey
    Project Editor: Gianna Williams
    Text Editor: Valerie Weber
    Designer: Ian Winton
    Cartographer: Stefan Chabluk
    Illustrators: Jim Channell, Stuart Lafford, Christian Webb

Marshall Cavendish
    Editor: Marian Armstrong
    Editorial Director: Paul Bernabeo

*(cover) Strawberry poison dart frog*

**Editor's Note:** Many systems of dating have been used by different cultures throughout history. *Rain Forests of the World* uses B.C.E. (Before Common Era) and C.E. (Common Era) instead of B.C. (Before Christ) and A.D. (Anno Domini, "In the Year of Our Lord") out of respect for the diversity of the world's peoples.

The publishers would like to thank the following for their permission to reproduce photographs:
486 David Cayless/Oxford Scientific Films, 487 Fred Hoogervorst/Panos Pictures, 488 Jean-Leo Dugast/Panos Pictures, 489 Bruce Herrod/OSF, 492 Michael Fogden/OSF, 493 Richard Davies/OSF, 494 Martin Wendler/Natural History Photographic Agency, 495 Susan Cunningham/Panos Pictures, 496 Corbis, 497 Fred Hoogervorst/Panos Pictures, 498 Konrad Wothe/OSF, 499 Panda/G. Tognon/Frank Lane Picture Agency, 500 Christer Fredriksson/Bruce Coleman, 502 Jerry Callow/Panos Pictures, 503 Partridge Films Ltd./OSF, 504 W. S. Clark/FLPA, 505 Michael Fogden/OSF, 506 M. Harvey/Foto Natura/FLPA, 507 Jules Cowan/Bruce Coleman, 508 K. G. Preston-Mafham/Premaphotos Wildlife, 509 Gerald S. Cubitt/Bruce Coleman, 510 Jeff Foott/Bruce Coleman, 511 Bruce Henry/FLPA, 512 Jany Sauvanet/NHPA, 513 Michael Fogden/OSF, 514 Nick Gordon/OSF, 515 A. N. T./NHPA, 516 Corbis, 517 K. G. Preston-Mafham/Premaphotos Wildlife, 518 Nick Gordon/OSF, 519 Dr. Ivan Polunin/NHPA, 521 Mark Newman/FLPA, 522 Patti Murray/OSF, 523 K. G. Preston-Mafham/Premaphotos Wildlife, 524 G. I. Bernard/NHPA, 525 Gerald S. Cubitt/Bruce Coleman, 526 Martin Harvey/NHPA, 527 Antonio Mazanares/Bruce Coleman, 528 & 529 K. G. Preston-Mafham/Premaphotos Wildlife, 530 James Carmichael Jr./NHPA, 531 Chris Mattison/FLPA, 532 Michael Fodgen/OSF, 533 Chris Mattison/FLPA, 535 Kevin Schafer/NHPA, 537 Luiz Claudio Marigo/Bruce Coleman, 538 Michael Powles/OSF, 539 Ken Preston-Mafham/Premaphotos Wildlife, 540 Philip Sharpe/OSF, 541 Dr. Ivan Polunin/NHPA, 542 Ken Preston-Mafham/Premaphotos Wildlife, 543 Daniel Heuclin/NHPA

**Library of Congress Cataloging-in-Publication Data**
Rain forests of the world.
                  v.  cm.
          Includes bibliographical references and index.
          Contents: v. 1. Africa–bioluminescence — v. 2. Biomass–clear-cutting — v. 3. Climate and weather–emergent — v. 4. Endangered species–food web — v. 5. Forest fire–iguana — v. 6. Indonesia–manatee — v. 7. Mangrove forest–orangutan — v. 8. Orchid–red panda — v. 9. Reforestation–spider — v. 10. Squirrel–Yanomami people — v. 11. Index.
                  ISBN 0-7614-7254-1 (set)
                      1. Rain forests—Encyclopedias.        1. Marshall Cavendish Corporation.
          QH86 .R39 2002
          578.734—dc21

    ISBN  0-7614-7254-1 (set)
    ISBN  0 7614-7263-0 (vol. 9)

Printed and bound in Italy

07 06 05 04 03 02 6 5 4 3 2 1

# Contents

Saving existing rain forests is crucial for the future of the planet, but what can be done with the vast areas of forest that have already been destroyed? These areas include those taken over by farmers and then abandoned when tropical rains washed away the topsoil. The remaining soil is often poor in nutrients or poisoned by chemical pesticides or fertilizers. New plant growth may begin, but will usually lack the rich variety of slow-growing hardwood trees and animal species that originally existed. After intensive plantation farming, the forest may take over a hundred years to recover naturally.

## KEY FACTS

● **Forest land cleared for farming may become useless within just three years of being cleared. Reforestation is the only way to restore value to the land.**

● **For every 10 trees cut down in tropical countries, only one new one is planted.**

● **An estimated 960 to 1,250 million acres (385 to 500 million hectares) of tropical land could be suitable for reforestation programs.**

The solution may be reforestation—an attempt to re-create the true rain forest environment by the managed planting of new trees. The restoration of forest benefits the land in many ways. New roots prevent further erosion of the landscape by tropical rains. As the new forest develops, it creates a rich environment that will attract wildlife.

### Who Replants the Forests?

Reforestation normally takes place for commercial reasons: to provide a sustainable source of marketable hardwood timber from a new, carefully managed forest. It may also take place for environmental reasons: to re-create a region's natural ecosystem. These two concerns need not compete with each other. Any attempt to re-create a natural environment that does not take regional economic needs into account may be doomed to failure.

The funding for reforestation may come from commercial forestry and logging or from

*East Africa has suffered from widespread deforestation. Acacia seedlings are being grown at this nursery for a reforestation program in Kenya.*

*Scientists tend seedlings at the Wanariset Research Institute for Sustainable Forestry in East Kalimantan.*

the fungi that grow in rain forest soils and see how they affect the other plants and trees. They need to understand plant diseases and other problems that may prevent successful reforestation, such as localized pollution from mining or farming.

Scientists need to investigate how particular wildlife species relate to tree species—insects may pollinate flowers, or birds and bats may spread seeds as they eat the fruits. These are nature's own reforesters and will play a part in the continued spread of the replanted forest.

international conservation groups and charities or government or international organizations such as the United Nations.

Reforestation can be costly, and it is often hard to complete major projects. It is difficult to accurately estimate how much investment will be required and what financial gains will result, and this may discourage private landowners from taking part in a project. International projects may be resisted by those national governments that resent outside interference.

In areas such as Australia and Central America, a lot of hard reforestation work has been done not by professional foresters but by conservation volunteers. Reforestation projects may involve teaching local schoolchildren about nursery, reforestation, and conservation techniques so that they can continue the work and safeguard the future.

### Reforestation Research

The first requirement for successful reforestation is scientific research into the rain forest ecosystem in general and of the biology of native tree species in particular. Scientists need to study soil samples and compare the area to be reforested with soil in surviving forest. They need to study

## IN FOCUS

# Fighting Global Warming

Forests perform an important job in absorbing carbon dioxide, one of the so-called greenhouse gases that blanket the planet and are believed to be responsible for global warming. Reforested areas are particularly useful, as young trees take in more carbon dioxide than old ones. One U.S. power company offered to plant 52 million new trees in Central America to balance the air pollution it creates. To make a major impact on the world's climate, however, tropical reforestation would have to take place on a vastly greater scale than it does now. Some experts say that over 1,300 million acres (525 million hectares) of land would be needed. Reforestation is not really an alternative to cutting the amount of carbon dioxide we pump into the air, just an additional—and very important—way of restoring balance to Earth's atmosphere.

Seeds of rare species must be collected and conserved under ideal conditions in seed banks. The conditions under which the seeds best germinate must be studied, as must the seedlings and their root systems. Light and shade are important considerations when growing seedlings and young plants, for the sunlight they receive in the wild varies greatly, depending on whether they are under the full canopy, in a clearing, or on the fringes of the forest. Processes that occur naturally must be followed carefully if humans are to mimic nature.

### Nurseries and Transplanting

Nurseries may be set up in or near the reforestation zone. A large reforestation project may need a base station where seed collection, storage, and propagation can take place, as well as smaller nurseries located throughout the region. Ideally these can be operated by local people, providing employment and training.

## IN FOCUS

## New Trees in Ecuador

It has been estimated that less than one percent of Ecuador's coastal rain forest has survived. Part of it is in the northwestern Mache range, where the 7,600-acre (3,000-hectare) Jatun Sacha Biological Station was founded in 1994. There, conservation volunteers help to grow about 100,000 new saplings every year for reforestation projects in the region. They grow some 140 species, many of them tropical fruit and nut trees.

The area required for cultivation is large, as tens of thousands of seedlings and cuttings may need to be raised at any one time. When a mahogany seedling reaches about 28 inches (70 cm) in height, it is bagged in soil for transplanting. Reforestation is a long-term process, as it will be at least 40 years or more before these hardwoods mature.

In the wild, many different tree species may be found in one hectare (2.5 acres) of rain forest—the record number discovered so far is 283, in Peru.

*Teak trees for the Southeast Asian rain forests are grown from seed at a nursery in Thailand.*

*Seedlings must be carefully tended, transplanted, and watered as they grow in the nursery. This can provide rewarding employment for local people.*

Nurseries therefore need to grow a wide variety of plant species. These must be planted on site so that they support each other's growth and development as they would naturally. Some trees rely on the leaf litter provided by others, for example. Fast-growing and slow-growing species must be balanced to control the shade and rainfall they receive.

The pattern of replanting is important for wildlife conservation. If reserves are small, their value can be greatly increased by planting corridors of growth, which join up surviving fragments of the original forest. Animals need to pass freely along the corridors in order to migrate or breed. The planting along riverbanks allows animals to drink or nest without breaking cover.

A major consideration in plant selection is economics. Managed commercial felling requires suitable species, and it is the profits from these that will pay for the initial costs of reforestation. The future forest stands a far better chance of survival if it benefits local people. Therefore species of native fruit and nut trees might be included so that they can be harvested for consumption or profit later on.

This may be seen as unnatural human interference, but it is nothing new. For thousands of years peoples in the Amazon rain forests have been propagating plants that are useful to them. Anthropologists can estimate historical populations in Amazonia because local populations practiced a kind of horticulture, planting nuts and seeds in places that would be convenient for the collection of fruit and nuts when the trees matured. The distribution of such trees today is a useful guide to past human habitation.

**Reforestation Worldwide**

Every reforestation project helps—every valley and coastal inlet, every bank and ridge, every small reserve and conservation area. However, the greatest impact on the global environment comes when reforestation takes place on a major scale, across a large region such as a whole river basin or major national park. In large areas there is less risk of animal populations becoming isolated and dying out and more chance of a rich variety of species being sustained.

## Check these out:
● **Clear-Cutting** ● **Conservation**
● **Deforestation** ● **Exploitation** ● **Human Interference**

Reptiles include turtles, tortoises, terrapins, lizards, snakes, and crocodiles. These all have one feature in common—they are covered in a tough and waterproof coat of scales that overlap one another. Reptiles evolved from amphibians many millions of years ago. Unlike amphibians, with their permanently damp skins, the scaly coats of reptiles are dry. Reptiles are cold-blooded animals, which means they are unable to regulate their own body temperature. For this reason, reptiles thrive in warmer climates, such as rain forests.

## KEY FACTS

● **Snakes molt their skin in one piece, but lizards shed theirs in flakes.**

● **Snakes can unhinge their jaws in order to swallow large prey whole.**

● **Except for most tortoises, which eat plants, reptiles are predators.**

## Nesting Habits

Compared to amphibians, reptiles are much less dependent on water, and many kinds rarely need to drink. Reptiles have also dispensed with the need for water in which to lay their eggs, which are hard-shelled and normally laid on land. Lizards lay from one to about 30 eggs, depending on species, size, and family. The young have a tiny egg tooth on the snout to help them hatch, which drops off soon after. In the rain forests of Southeast Asia the king cobra may be found coiled on top of its eggs, laid in a large mound of dead leaves. Unlike most other snakes, the king cobra guards its eggs, and the warmth of its body probably helps them hatch faster. The females of most pythons also coil

## RAIN FOREST REPTILES

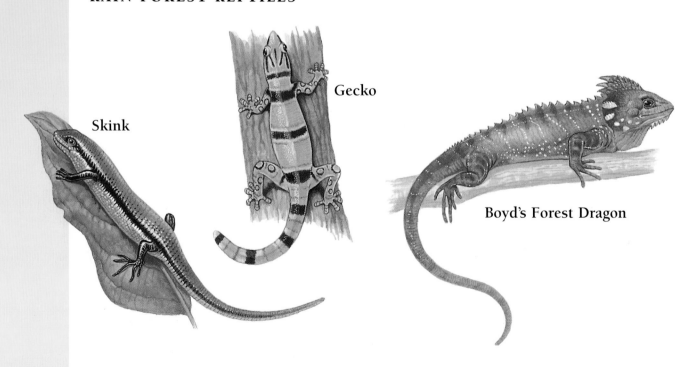

Skink

Gecko

Boyd's Forest Dragon

their bodies around their eggs and wait until they hatch. Female crocodiles usually dig nests on riverbanks, and in some species the female sits on guard nearby until the babies hatch, when they may be carried safely to the nearest water in the mother's mouth. Many lizards and snakes do not lay eggs, but retain them within their bodies and give birth to live young.

## Male and Female

Male and female reptiles are rarely matched in size: among most lizards, tortoises, and crocodilians, males are bigger than females; among most snakes and certain aquatic tortoises, females are bigger than males. Sometimes male and female reptiles differ only slightly, but in some lizards the difference can be very conspicuous. For example, many male chameleons have nose-mounted horns and different coloration than females. Male nose-horned lizards from Sri Lanka have a prominent white horn projecting from the

## The Madagascan Leaf-Tailed Gecko

When it comes to the art of sitting invisibly on the trunk of a tree, the Madagascan leaf-tailed gecko is the world's foremost expert. Its disappearing trick is no easy matter, for this is one of the world's largest geckos, up to 12 in. (30 cm) long, so there is a lot of gecko to hide. Its main ruse is to lie absolutely still and press itself tightly against the bark. Along the lower edges of the body, and especially beneath the rather deep jaw, there is a broad frill of skin that hangs down against the bark. The frill's job is to make an invisible, seamless join between lizard and tree. The gecko's second line of defense lies in shock tactics. If suddenly touched, it rears its head up and opens its mouth to reveal a startling crimson tongue.

tip of their noses, while the females just have the merest suggestion of a point.

Eyelash Palm Pit Viper

Hinge-Backed Tortoise

Dwarf Crocodile

## Basking

Like amphibians, and unlike the warm-blooded mammals and birds, reptiles are cold-blooded, which means that they cannot generate their own internal heat. In order to warm up, reptiles have to bask in the sun. One big advantage of letting the sun do all the work of generating body heat is that reptiles need far less food than warm-blooded creatures, which use up part of their food supplies just to stay warm.

Male anole lizards have a flap of skin called a dewlap tucked away beneath their chin. The concealed folds of this dewlap are brightly colored in red, blue, white, or yellow and can be abruptly extended downward in a spectacular way to form a brilliant fan. The males use these dewlap displays in territorial disputes with other males and to attract females. Many male lizards adopt bright colors only during the breeding season, such as the garishly flamboyant heads of the chisel-teeth lizards. In some species these bright and conspicuous dress colors can rapidly fade away at will, reverting quickly to the usual drab camouflage that is always worn by the females.

### Using Camouflage

Camouflage is the main defensive strategy employed by many reptiles in the rain forests, although some species, such as the highly poisonous coral snakes, adopt bright patterns called warning colors. Most lizards that spend their lives on tree trunks are colored so that they blend in well with the bark. Even some snakes, such as the lichen (LIE-kuhn) viper of Central America, spend the day in a camouflaged pose on tree bark, pressing their coiled bodies tightly against the wood so as to blend in perfectly. Some rain forest snakes and lizards are green and spend the day among leaves, making them very difficult to spot unless they betray their position by moving.

Another method of defense is employed by many lizards when they are suddenly attacked. They shed their tails, which wriggle and thrash about all by themselves, distracting the attacker's attention while the tail's former owner scoots away to safety. The lizard

*The poison of the fer–de–lance quickly renders its prey immobile. In this case the unlucky victim is a lizard caught on the rain forest floor in Costa Rica.*

*The jagged edge of the shell on the spiny hill tortoise from Southeast Asia makes the turtle hard to spot among the dead leaves on the rain forest floor. The spines probably make it difficult for snakes to swallow it.*

can afford to lose its tail—rather than its life—and a new tail will eventually grow to replace the old one. However, the substitute is never as fine or long as the original.

Tortoises and turtles are protected by their tough shells, which are often highly domed in terrestrial species but flatter and more streamlined in aquatic species. The shells of some species are armed with spines, especially in the young, which are more vulnerable to attack. Young spiny forest turtles from Southest Asia are extremely difficult for predators to swallow.

Many snakes, such as the gaboon viper from Africa and the fer-de-lance from

Central and South America, lie coiled up on the ground, where they resemble a pile of dead leaves. They sometimes lie on paths, although the chances of accidentally stepping on one are very remote. Despite their camouflage, snakes are easily spotted by snake-eating eagles, which swoop down and grab the reptile behind its head with a pair of strong and sharp talons. When this happens, the snake is usually doomed. Although the deadliest snakes are able to inject poison through hollow fangs, the fangs are of little use against the densely feathered legs of their attackers.

## Check these out:
● Camouflage ● Chameleon ● Crocodile and Caiman ● Gecko ● Iguana ● Lizard ● Snake ● Turtle and Terrapin

493

# Resettlement

In some tropical countries there are huge problems of poverty and overcrowding in the cities. Vast tracts of rain forest land seem to provide an ideal solution. In parts of South America, Asia, and Africa, governments have introduced resettlement programs by which they move homeless or jobless people from the cities to begin a new life in the country. But although this goes some way toward reducing city populations, resettlement creates a whole new set of serious problems.

## KEY FACTS

● **There are two main types of resettlement programs: moving city people into the rain forest, and relocating rain forest peoples to make way for development.**

● **There are just over one million indigenous people living in the Amazon rain forest today, compared to around 8 million in 1500 C.E.**

● **In the last 20 years, 24 million Brazilian farmers have been forced off their land as part of rain forest colonization programs.**

## Moving People In

The first resettlement programs began in the 1950s in Angola and Southeast Asia. Millions of new settlers were tempted by rain forest land that had been cleared of trees—or that they had to clear for themselves—for farming. Rain forests are so rich with animal and plant life that it is easy to see why the settlers believed they would be able to use the land to farm, either growing crops or raising livestock on pastureland. However, the rich layer of humus that carpets a rain forest floor is formed by dead leaves from the trees and by the droppings of the wide variety of forest animals. Once the trees are gone, the wildlife leaves or dies, and there are no fresh nutrients to enrich the soil.

Without tree roots to hold it together, the soil easily washes away in the daily downpours. Within a few seasons, the soil becomes poor and thin, crops fail, and settlers face starvation and death. They are often unable to return to the city, because they would have to return the money they received as part of the resettlement package. This forces many of

*This Brazilian woman and her family were encouraged to move to a small farm in the Amazon rain forest.*

*Workers pan for gold in a Brazilian gold mine. Unfortunately, areas of rain forest in the Amazon basin that are cleared for mining will never grow back.*

**Effects on Rain Forest People**
Of course, it is not only the settlers who face problems as a result of the resettlement. Rain forest people often find their traditional way of life changed forever. For example, the Machiguenga live in remote rain forest areas in southeast Peru. Since the 1970s, farmers have moved in to grow crops of coffee and cocoa. In the past, the Machiguenga lived by hunting animals, catching fish, and growing crops such as sugarcane or manioc in small forest clearings. Today, many Machiguenga grow cash crops instead, which they sell to buy Western-style goods. As a result, their old knowledge of how to use the rain forest in a sustainable way is fast disappearing.

Other local peoples trade with the settlers for guns. This results in the loss of traditional hunting techniques. More animals can be caught

them to abandon their farms to find new land, moving deeper into the rain forest and felling more trees. The land they leave behind will have become completely barren, and rain forest cannot regrow there.

Soil quality is not the only problem. Settlers have to face hostility or even violent attacks from local forest peoples who resent losing their traditional hunting grounds. There are invisible threats, too. Mosquitoes and other biting insects carry deadly tropical diseases such as malaria and dengue fever. Unpurified water contains parasites that transmit other diseases. Forest peoples often have a natural immunity to these diseases because, unlike the new settlers, they have been exposed to them all their lives. For the settlers, far from civilization, a doctor might be more than a day's journey away through the dense forest.

**IN FOCUS**

## Violent Clashes in Indonesia

In Indonesia, the fourth-most populated country in the world, there have been many clashes between the indigenous Dyak people and settlers. In February 2001, Dyaks on the island of Borneo killed nearly 500 Madurese people and forced 50,000 more to leave their homes. The problem arose because of serious overcrowding on the Indonesian islands of Bali, Java, Madura, and Timor. The government resettlement program offers people free land, housing, and food aid to move to rain forest areas.

# Compensating the Panara

In December 1997 a court forced the Brazilian government to pay compensation to the Panara people of Mato Grosso. The Panara had been forced to resettle in Xingu National Park because their hunting grounds were being cleared to build a huge new highway. As a result of contact with other peoples, the Panara were exposed to diseases to which they had no immunity. Over just three years, nearly 200 people died of influenza and diarrhea. The Panara lived in the national park between the early 1970s and the mid-1990s, when they were finally allowed to return to their land, even though it had been radically altered by the building work.

and killed, so many more species become endangered. Settlers affect the people in other ways, too. Rain forest land and water supplies that adjoin their farmsteads may be damaged by pesticides and fertilizers.

## Cheap Labor

Not all government resettlement programs offer the independence of owning a small farmstead. Some encourage poor people from the cities to work for the big businesses that are clearing the rain forests. This may involve logging and clearing the land itself, but there are also many

other industries that require cheap, government-subsidized labor. In Malaysia, the Philippines, and also many parts of South America, rubber plantations need tappers. In Thailand, people are sent to mine for precious jewels such as emeralds and rubies, and across the Amazon basin, gold mining offers work to the poor. Other resettlement projects need workers to construct services for these industries— new roads, hydroelectric dams that produce electrical power, or pipelines that carry oil, all of which involve clearing thousands of acres of precious rain forest land.

## Moving People Out

As well as moving people in to clear the rain forests, other resettlement programs move rain forest peoples out or to small enclaves of forest, for example to national parks or reserves. This happens when their homeland is taken over by big business. If local peoples are not resettled, the result is usually violence. Across Africa and Asia, eucalyptus plantations are replacing rain forest areas in order to supply the paper industry, and this forces

*These Miskito Indians from coastal Nicaragua are being relocated to a camp. Their rain forest home was cleared for plantations and then ravaged by hurricanes.*

local people to resettle elsewhere. Other big businesses include large-scale ranching or mining. Industrial-scale mining is far more damaging to the rain forests than the activities of resettled farmers.

For local peoples, resettlement can have both good and bad effects. In Malaysia, for example, Iban people were resettled to make way for a huge hydroelectric dam. In their new homes, the people had basic modern amenities such as fresh water and electricity for the first time in their lives, as well as access to schools and clinical care. However, the Iban were not given enough new land to be self-sufficient, so they lost their independence. They also need to find money to pay for the new amenities. This means they are forced to work on local rubber or oil palm plantations, often for very low wages. Different groups of rain forest peoples are often mixed together in the new settlements, resulting in the loss of mother languages and in the spread of disease. Rain forest peoples originally lived in isolated communities. When they come into contact with new people, they encounter diseases to which they have no natural immunity.

### Compensation

Recently governments have been forced to compensate local peoples whose lives were badly affected by resettlement projects. Governments have been forced to pay compensation because of world opinion and the actions of pressure groups, and in

*The Indonesian government has encouraged people on its most crowded islands to move to Borneo. The people live in settlements like this one in the province of Kalimantan. However, settlers often face violence from indigenous peoples.*

some instances because of legal action brought by local peoples themselves or by people acting for them.

Campaigns by local peoples for rights to their traditional lands are also slowing projects in places such as the Amazon basin. As people are granted ownership of the land, with title deeds that are recognized in courts of law, it becomes impossible for others to be resettled there from the city. Unfortunately, rain forest peoples are still being moved so that development can continue. Even if they are given compensation, the money soon runs out, and the people can no longer rely on the rain forest to supply their needs.

## Check these out:
● Disease  ● Dyak People  ● Exploitation
● Mining  ● Miskito People  ● Oil
Exploration  ● People of the Rain Forest

497

Of the five species of rhinoceros, only the Javan and Sumatran rhinos live in rain forests. Once widespread, they are now very limited in their distribution and are classed as endangered. A third species, the Indian rhino, lives primarily in wet grassland but also ventures into the adjacent monsoon forest to feed.

The Javan rhino has a head-and-body length of up to 11½ feet (3.5 m) and can weigh up to 3,500 pounds (1,600 kg), while the Sumatran rhino is a little smaller, with a head-and-body length of between 8 and 9 feet (2.5 and 2.8 m) and weighing up to 2,200 pounds (1,000 kg). The Javan rhino has one horn and the Sumatran two. Both are browsers, feeding on vegetation using a prehensile upper lip that can twist around branches and leaves.

### The Javan Rhino

The Javan rhino once lived from Assam and Bangladesh, through Thailand and Vietnam (where half a dozen still survive), and down the Malaysian peninsula to the islands of Sumatra and Java. It was originally killed because it damaged crops, but it was hunted for medicinal purposes as well. The last Javan rhino in Myanmar was shot in 1920, and in peninsular Malaysia in 1932; the species was extinct in Sumatra by the mid-1940s. It survives on Java only in Ujung-Kulon National Park, at the western tip of the island, where there may be as few as 50 individuals. The Javan rhino has been known to push over trees as thick as 3½ inches (9 cm) in diameter to reach the parts it wants to eat.

### The Sumatran Rhino

The Sumatran rhino is a solitary animal, spending most of its time hiding in thick cover and emerging only in the evenings and the early mornings to eat leaves, twigs, bamboo shoots, and fallen fruits such as wild mangoes and figs.

This rhino, which once lived alongside the Javan rhino throughout its range except on Java, has a very similar history to the Javan. It was hunted mainly for its horns, used in traditional Asian medicines, and now survives only in three countries: Myanmar, Sumatra, and Malaysia. Its total world population is now about 300 individuals.

*The Sumatran rhino is the most primitive species, with a hairy coat and a fringe of whiskers around its ears, features that have been lost by more modern species.*

## Check these out:

⬤ Endangered Species ⬤ Herbivore
⬤ Indonesia ⬤ Mammal

# River

Rain forests cover areas with very high rainfall levels. On average, rain forests require around 80 inches (2,000 mm) of rain per year, and it may be up to three times this amount in some areas. However, in parts of western Africa rainfall can be as little as 48-60 inches (1,200-1,500 mm) per year. In some areas of forest there is little variation in the monthly rainfall, while in monsoon forest there are pronounced wet and dry

seasons. With very high rainfall comes a great deal of water to be carried away from the forest by rivers.

Even with just 80 inches (2,000 mm) of rain each year, each square mile of forest (2.6 km²) receives 1,350 million gallons (5 billion liters) of water on it during that time. The rain forest rivers, therefore, have to move enormous quantities of water down to the world's oceans. The world's greatest river system is the Amazon and its tributaries. Around 50,000 miles (80,000 km) of the rivers in the Amazon basin can be navigated by boats, and there are a further 500,000 miles (800,000 km) of smaller rivers and streams. On an average day these empty more than 50 million gallons (190 million liters) of water per second into the Atlantic Ocean. The result of this huge outflow is that for many miles out from the Amazon's 200-mile- (320-km-) wide delta, the water is not salty but fresh.

The size and extent of rain forest rivers vary enormously, with the Amazon and its

*A tributary of the mighty Amazon River meandering through the forest. A number of oxbow lakes, no longer joined to the river, are clearly visible.*

499

*Wet foliage with epiphytic plants overhang a small river running through a rain forest in Sumatra.*

tributaries making up the largest system, draining an area the size of Europe. This is followed by the Congo and its tributaries, which drain an area in West and Central Africa roughly one third of that of the Amazon basin.

### White- and Black-Water Rivers

Most of the world's rain forest rivers originate in mountainous or hilly areas and then flow down through the rain forest. Other water comes from rain draining off the main lowland rain forest. The nature and origins of rivers have a noticeable effect upon the type of forest that surrounds them.

There are two different types of rain forest rivers, the white-water river and the black-water river. White-water rivers come from hills or mountains where the rocks are weathering fairly fast and release lots of minerals into their waters. Black-water rivers, however, come from areas of rock that are breaking down fairly slowly, and they therefore do not contain much in the way of minerals. White-water rivers will support a much richer plant and animal life than black-water

rivers. Also, when the white-water rivers flood, as many rain forest rivers do for at least some part of the year, they provide the surrounding forest with a rich source of nutrients for plant growth. As a result of these differences, the dominant tree species that grow in black-water river regions differ from those in white-water river areas. This in turn has an effect on which plants and animals will live there.

In some areas, especially in parts of the Amazon basin, the forest is flooded seasonally for a number of weeks. As a result, there tend to be fewer different species of trees living there, for they have to be adapted to withstand a long period when the soil is waterlogged.

### Life Along the Rivers

Like rivers anywhere, those of the rain forests are homes for the animals and plants that live in and alongside them. Where the smaller streams and rivers are overhung by trees and little light reaches the water, plants tend to be scarce. As the rivers broaden out, however, the number of water and waterside plants increases. Where the rivers are slow, or where they have formed oxbow lakes due to a change in their course, which often happens following flooding, they may be covered in water lilies or water hyacinths, while the banks may be covered in waterside grasses.

Rivers provide a source of water for larger mammals and birds, which come down to drink at the water's edge. Riverbanks also supply water and salts for many of the forest butterflies, which may often gather there in large numbers to drink. Numerous species of fish, including many of the brightly colored species that may find their way into tropical fish tanks in developed countries,

### IN FOCUS

## A Multitude of Fish

Rain forest rivers contain an enormous variety of fish species. More than 230 species have been identified from one relatively small area of the Congo basin. Even more impressive is the Amazon basin. More than 5,000 fish species have been identified from there, with more yet to be discovered. This is about the same number of species as are known to live in the Atlantic Ocean.

*Two forest dwellers pole their canoe across the Congo as it meanders through the rain forest in the Democratic Republic of the Congo.*

thrive there. These in turn act as food for larger fish, otters, crocodilians, and the many birds that live along the rivers. The smaller streams act as breeding areas for a number of species of frogs and toads, while the many sandbanks along the broader rivers provide places in which turtles and terrapins can bask and lay their eggs. Otters, hippopotamus, and dugongs may be found in the rivers of the Congo basin, while river dolphins live in the white-water rivers of the Amazon basin.

## Peoples of the Rivers

The rivers of the rain forest attract people who live alongside them and make much of their livelihood from them. The waters of the rivers provide them with food in the form of fish, frogs, crayfish, and turtles. Fishing may be carried out in a number of different ways. Amazon River people catch fish with throw nets, impale them using bows and arrows, or stun them in smaller streams and rivers by poisoning the water. Poison is also used in the Congo system. Other groups build fish traps, usually where there are rapids in the river. People also bathe in the rivers and obtain drinking water from them. Not all of the riverside peoples build canoes or boats, but for those who do the rivers also act as highways through the rain forest.

### IN FOCUS

## Dams

As the towns and cities in rain forest areas of the world increase in size and their citizens become more wealthy, so the need for electricity increases. The simple way to do this is to dam the rain forest rivers, for they contain huge quantities of water capable of producing enormous amounts of electricity. Brazil, for example, has plans for 22 dams in the Amazon basin by the year 2010, which will flood around 92,000 sq. mi. (240,000 km²) of rain forest, an area roughly the size of the state of Colorado.

## Check these out:
- Biodiversity ● Dolphin ● Fish
- Fishing ● Flooding ● Hydroelectricity
- Water ● Watershed

# Rodent

Rodents are smallish mammals whose teeth and mouths are adapted for gnawing. Many species feed on nuts, seeds, and other hard food. They in turn are food for many of the forests' carnivores, both large and small. Rodents include mice, rats, squirrels, porcupines, guinea pigs, agoutis (uh-GOO-tees), pacas, and capybaras. All have just one pair of incisors (the front teeth), which are very sharp for cutting and gnawing.

The incisors keep growing throughout the rodent's life to compensate for the hard wear. If rodents do not have enough hard food to gnaw on, as sometimes happens in captivity, the teeth may grow so long that it becomes impossible for the animal to eat; they may even grow up into the skull, causing death. Rodents can move their lower jaw into two different positions: one brings the front teeth together for gnawing, while the other brings the large, flatter cheek teeth (molars) together for chewing and grinding.

Behind the incisors in each jaw is a gap with no teeth called the diastema (die-uh-STEE-muh). The rodent can suck its cheeks into this gap to prevent chips of nuts and other sharp objects from getting into its mouth as it gnaws.

*The pacas of Central and South America are particularly fond of mangoes and avocados. They come out at night to forage near rivers and ponds.*

# World's Largest Rodent

Capybaras (ka-pih-BAR-uhs) are the largest living rodents. Related to guinea pigs, they have blunt noses, barrel-shaped bodies, no tails, long legs, and slightly webbed toes. Capybaras are grazing animals that live in herds of 40 or more, headed by a large male. They feed mainly on waterside grasses and aquatic plants. Capybaras can stay under water for almost five minutes. Their nostrils, eyes, and ears are at the top of their large heads, so they can swim along almost totally submerged and still breathe, see, and hear.

## Varied Diets

Most rodents are vegetarians. They particularly like to eat nuts and seeds, which they hold with their front paws while feeding. Many rodents, such as the agouti of South America, have cheek pouches in which they can carry seeds back to their nests. Fruits, berries, and young shoots are also popular meals. The capybaras, pacas, and agoutis of South America are grazers, feeding mainly on leaves, stems, and fruits. The capybara will stand half submerged in water while it feeds on aquatic grasses.

Porcupines feed on leaves, buds, bark, and twigs, and Old World porcupines will also eat carrion. A few rodents, such as the Australian water rat, which eats fish, frogs, and mollusks, are carnivores. Many rodents supplement their plant diet with insects and spiders.

## Running, Climbing, Flying

The guinea pigs, pacas, agoutis, and capybaras of South American rain forests are expert runners. They walk and run on the tips of their toes, and their nails have become like little hooves. With only a small area of their feet touching the ground, there is not much friction, so they can run fast.

Many rain forest rodents, including rats, mice, squirrels, and porcupines, can climb trees. This gives them access to a larger food supply—nuts, seeds, and fruits—and it keeps them out of reach of ground-dwelling predators and, in some forests, floods. Most climbing rodents use their short, curved claws to cling to the bark.

Squirrels can swivel their ankles so that they can climb down trees headfirst, using the claws on their hind feet as a brake. The big toes of palm mice, tree mice, and forest rats are opposable: they can be moved opposite the other toes to grasp twigs and branches. Many tree dwellers use their tail for balancing while running along branches. The tail also acts as both rudder and parachute when the animal leaps from branch to branch. Some species have flattened tails, which they press against tree trunks for extra support.

If a small rodent has to descend to the ground to get from one tree to another, it may be in great danger. Several groups of squirrels all around the world have evolved ways of gliding from tree to tree. Flying squirrels have thick fur-covered membranes of skin stretching along the sides of their bodies from their wrists to their ankles. The squirrel launches itself from a branch or tree trunk and stretches out its arms and legs, spreading out its gliding membrane like a parachute to swoop down to the next tree trunk. African scaly-tailed squirrels have a gliding membrane attached to a long, slender piece of cartilage that grows out from the elbow. These squirrels and some climbing rats have spiny scales under the tips of their tails, which act as both climbing aids and antiskid devices.

## Aquatic Rodents

The water rats of Australia, New Guinea, and South America hunt for small invertebrates and fish in the lakes, ponds, and streams of the rain forests. Their fur is dense and waterproof. Their feet are webbed for swimming and for walking on soft mud. They swim by kicking with their large, webbed feet. Other swamp rats have fringes of stiff hairs on their toes and sometimes their tails, too, instead of webs.

*This naked–tailed climbing rat from Costa Rica has large hind feet with strong claws for climbing trees.*

Rats that live in marshy areas, such as the African swamp rats, have long, spreading hind feet, so they do not sink in the soft mud. The capybara of South America has webbed feet. It dives into the water at the first hint of danger and may stay under water for several minutes, all the time moving farther away from danger.

## Retreats and Defenses

Most small rodents make burrows in the ground or among tree roots, or they nest in tree holes out of sight of predators. The tiny pencil-tailed tree mouse of Asian rain forests nests inside the stems of bamboos. Other mice and rats use old birds' nests or fallen corn cobs. Javan flying squirrels will nest in half-eaten coconuts, while African porcupines may set up house in termite mounds.

Not all rodents live alone. Some mice and rats live in large social groups that have strict pecking orders.

The burrow or nest hole is the first line of retreat when threatened. Voles make tunnels in the grass along regular routes to feeding areas so that they can make a quick escape. If safety is too far away, the rodent may freeze, relying on its inconspicuous colors to blend into the background. Some squirrels have striped coats that mimic the shafts of sunlight streaming through the trees. Like some lizards, a few rats and mice can shed their tails to help them escape.

## Food or Foe?

Small rodents can multiply rapidly, producing up to 13 litters of young a year, and their young can reproduce when only five or six weeks old. Rodents are food for many rain forest animals, especially hawks, owls, cats, and foxes. Humans also eat them. Guinea pig is a common dish in parts of South America, and capybaras are farmed in many areas.

However, rodents can also destroy human food. Rats and mice pillage stores in rain forest villages. In Asia, rice field rats eat seedlings and young shoots of rice, while in West Africa and Malaysia rats love to eat the hearts of young oil palms. Coconuts, dates, corn, coffee, cocoa beans, melons, and citrus fruits all fall prey to the appetites of rodents.

## IN FOCUS

# Prickly Porcupines

Porcupines are large, rather slow-moving rodents, covered in stiff quills (modified hairs). The tree porcupine, or coendou, of Central and South America (below) has a specially adapted prehensile tail that can curl around branches like a fifth limb. It has hard, bare skin on the upper surface of the tip of its tail: the part that grips the branch. Porcupines excel at defense. The crested porcupine of Africa can rattle its quills to warn off an attacker. If this does not work, it may then run backward into the predator, impaling it on the quills. The tips of the quills break off, leaving irritant wounds. Quills of the brush-tailed porcupines from Africa and Asia are coated in little scales that can carry infections into the wounds, which can prove fatal.

Many rodents carry serious human diseases, such as plague, typhus, salmonella, and Lassa fever. They may well cause more deaths than all the human wars put together.

## Check these out:
● Disease ● Food Web ● Locomotion
● Mammal ● Squirrel

506

Roots are a plant's means of absorbing water and minerals from the soil. There are more different kinds of roots in tropical rain forests than anywhere else on Earth.

With the heavy tropical rain, nutrients tend to get washed out of the soil. The greatest concentrations of nutrients are close to the soil surface, where they are released as the leaf litter rots. The great forest trees often have roots at two levels: nutrient-gathering feeder roots near the soil surface that also trap rainwater before it drains away through the soil, and deeper roots that anchor the tree. The forest floor is crisscrossed with curious buttress roots, prop roots, and the trailing roots of strangler figs.

## KEY FACTS

● **Just behind the tip of a root are many fine hairlike cells—the root hairs. Combined, these have an enormous surface area for absorbing water and dissolved minerals.**

● **Many forest trees have fungi surrounding their roots or even inside them, which take up nutrients for them.**

● **The root of *Derris*, a woody climber from Southeast Asia, contains a poison used as insecticide, flea powder, and arrow-tip poison.**

### Roots in the Air

When rain forest trees suffer from water shortage or lack of nutrients, new roots may grow down, sideways, or even upward along the tree trunks. In the moist humid atmosphere, these aerial roots are not at risk of drying out. Epiphytic plants such as orchids and bromeliads (broe-MEE-lee-ads), which grow on the branches and trunks of other plants, send out roots to trap moisture and dissolved nutrients that trickle over the bark of the host tree.

The roots of many orchids are coated in a spongelike tissue—called velamen—that can absorb moisture from the air. This tissue is made up of dead cells that have many tiny holes in their walls to let water in. When full of water, these cells become transparent and the greenish

*The roots of these tall forest trees in Olympic National Park, Washington State, envelop the fallen tree that supported them as seedlings.*

inner tissues show through. The water absorbed by the velamen is transported to the rest of the orchid plant. When dry, the velamen cells appear white. They reflect light, so the root absorbs less heat and less water is lost from it by evaporation.

The leaf bases of epiphytic ferns such as the staghorn fern, bird's nest fern, and bracket fern overlap to form a kind of basket that traps leaf litter. This rots to form a nutrient-rich soil at the base of the fern, which also helps to trap moisture. A mesh of fine roots grows out into this soil to absorb the moisture and nutrients, making an even better trap.

## Special Partnerships

The roots of most plants grow downward. Special chemical messengers called auxins respond to the force of gravity and cause

---

## IN FOCUS

# Breathing Roots

In swampy, waterlogged soil, underground roots cannot get enough oxygen. Many mangrove trees and other swamp forest trees produce pneumatophores that rise out of the mud like knobbly knees. They have lots of little pores (tiny holes) called lenticels in the bark to let oxygen in. Other mangroves produce a dense tangle of arching prop roots. These also help to trap mud washed in by rivers or tides. The mud builds up, forming new land and making the soil drier, so different species of mangrove plants can invade.

---

the root cells to expand more on the side away from the pull of gravity, so the root curves downward.

Cycads (SIE-kuhds)—palmlike conifers found from Africa to Asia and Australia—have thick, fleshy roots that can shrink, or contract, to pull the stem deeper into the ground. However, some of their roots grow toward the surface of the soil. These roots are knobbly and branching, like corals, and are called coralloid roots. They contain cyanobacteria—bacteria that can trap nitrogen from the air and convert it into nitrogen compounds, which they pass to the cycad.

Many plants, especially forest trees, form close associations with certain fungi (FUN-jie), which may live inside or wrapped around their roots. The fungi take up nutrients from the soil, modify them, and pass them to the plant.

*Aerial roots fan out from the leaf bases of this philodendron from the Central American cloud forest. They will cling to any support they find.*

Some climbing plants, such as peperomias (peh-puh-ROE-mee-uhs), send out short suckerlike roots to cling to tree trunks. Others, like Swiss-cheese plants and bauhinias (boe-hin-EE-uhs), have adventitious roots (roots that arise from stems) that cling to the trunks of trees. Strangler figs use a different tactic. Starting life as a seedling on a branch high in the forest canopy, they send out roots that grow all the way down to the forest floor hundreds of feet below. There, they compete with their host's roots for nutrients. Their shoots fan out, shade the host's shoot, and reduce its ability to photosynthesize. Eventually the host tree dies, and the strangler fig's roots, now woody, form a meshlike hollow trunk to support it.

## Extra Support

Some of the very tall rain forest trees have strange roots that take the form of buttresses radiating out from the main trunk. These buttress roots are 3 to 4 inches (8 to 10 cm) thick and may rise up to 9 feet (3 m) above the ground and extend 16$\frac{1}{2}$ feet (5 m) from the main trunk. They are thought to help anchor the tree by spreading its weight over a larger area of ground. Buttress roots are often more developed on the windward side of a tree. If its buttresses are cut away, a tree will usually fall down.

Particularly common on wet, swampy soils, buttresses form by growing upward from roots near the soil surface. Leaf litter gets trapped among the buttresses,

providing the trees with more nutrients. The buttresses send down fine feeder roots to tap these nutrients. Many animals make their homes in the hollows between buttresses. These roots also provide a large surface area for climbers to start their growth up the tree.

*The strong buttress roots of this* Intsia *tree from Madagascar help support the tree and trap rotting leaves, which provide extra nutrients.*

Other trees, such as the red mangrove, gain extra support with adventitious roots that grow out of the trunk some way above the ground and arch down into the soil, branching into many side roots as they near the ground. These prop roots act like a tripod to support the tree. They are particularly common on palms and in mangrove forests.

509

## Edible and Inedible

Just as potatoes and carrots are common foods in temperate climates, so the roots of some tropical plants are important food crops. The roots of some tropical plants swell up with stored nutrients. Yams are a staple food in Africa and parts of Southeast Asia. They will keep for months if properly stored, so are vital starch-rich foods in times of drought.

Cassava, or manioc, is a staple food in many parts of the Tropics. It is made from the root tubers of *Manihot* species, small shrubs or trees of the spurge family native to the Americas. Each tuber may weigh up to 30 pounds (14 kg). Cassava flour is made into bread or tapioca, cassava cakes in Yucatán, Mexico, bami mush in Jamaica, and the gelatinous fufu in West Africa. Cassava starch was probably first extracted by the Maya in Yucatán. In most varieties of *Manihot*, the tubers contain cyanide, a lethal poison. Cassava poison is powerful enough to be used in poison arrows and

*Prop roots arch down from the trunks of these red mangroves, absorbing oxygen from the air as well as helping to anchor the trees in the mud.*

darts. However, rain forest people have evolved a long treatment process of grating, pressing, and heating these roots to remove the poison.

Other starch-rich roots contain certain chemicals to deter animals from eating them. The root of ipecacuanha (ih-puh-KAK-yuh-wah-nah), from Brazil, is an important drug used to treat dysentery. The roots of *Derris* species, woody climbers from many parts of the Tropics, especially Southeast Asia, contain insect-killing chemicals, which are widely used in commercial insecticides and flea-powders. Locals use them as fish poisons and arrow-tip poisons.

### IN FOCUS

## Root or Leaf?

Some epiphytic orchids have hardly any leaves. Instead, their long roots carry out photosynthesis just like a leaf. When wet, these roots appear green, as the green inner tissues show through the transparent velamen. An example is *Taeniophyllum*, species of which are found in Africa, Asia, and the Pacific region. It has no leaves at all, and its roots are green and ribbonlike. Its Latin name means "tapeworm leaf."

## Check these out:

● Climber ● Emergent ● Food ● Forest Floor ● Mangrove Forest ● Nutrient Cycle ● Plant ● Tree

For thousands of years rubber was known only to the hunter-gatherers of the Amazon rain forest. It is produced naturally by trees, the most important of which is the Brazilian rubber tree *Hevea brasiliensis*. It was used by native South Americans for making waterproof shoes and coats long before Columbus arrived in the New World in 1492, but Europeans thought of it as nothing more than a curiosity for more than two hundred years. In 1736 a French explorer, Charles de la Condamine, sent some rolls of crude rubber home with a list of the things made from it by the people of the Amazon forests, and gradually a market for it began to grow in Europe. For another 140 years the only source of rubber was wild trees in the South American forests. It was not cultivated elsewhere in the world until 1876.

Rows of trees in plantations are much easier to harvest than wild trees scattered all over the forest. Soon there were plantations all around the eastern Tropics, and today 95 percent of all natural rubber comes from Southeast Asia. There are some plantations in West Africa, for example in Cameroon, Nigeria, and Liberia, where the damp tropical climate is suitable.

**KEY FACTS**

● First extracted from a plant known only to Amazon rain forest dwellers, rubber is now used all over the world.

● Three-quarters of the rubber used in the world today is synthetic.

● Almost all natural rubber comes from Southeast Asia, where it is grown in plantations.

*Tapping rubber in Sri Lanka. A new groove is cut below a series of old ones after the flow in the last groove has stopped.*

511

*Diagonal cuts in the rubber tree bark produce a faster flow of latex than the more traditional method, but after the flow stops they cannot be recut as quickly.*

## Harvesting Rubber

Rubber is collected by tapping, making a diagonal cut about halfway around the bark of the tree. The milky latex that flows from the cut is then collected in a small cup attached to the trunk. When the flow stops, usually in the second day, the first cut is extended by slicing another strip of bark from below it. Each tapping produces about 1 fluid ounce (30 ml) of latex. When the cuts reach the ground, the tree is allowed to heal before the process is repeated. A rubber plantation with 100 trees per acre (250 per hectare) can produce 400 pounds per acre (450 kg per hectare), though special high-yielding trees have been bred that can produce as much as 3,000 pounds per acre (3,400 kg per hectare).

The latex is strained to remove lumps and insects, diluted with water, and treated with acid, which makes the rubber particles stick together. Then it is rolled into thin sheets and dried before being rolled up for shipment. Further treatment usually involves vulcanization, in which the raw rubber is cooked with sulfur to make it stronger and more elastic. It also gives it a better grip on dry surfaces, making it suitable for tires.

The growth of rubber plantations during the 20th century was amazingly fast. In 1900 there were 5,000 acres (2,000 hectares) in the whole world; at the last complete count in 1996 there were 15.6 million acres (6.3 million hectares). However, plantations are vulnerable to the weather: if it is too wet, the trees do not produce suitable latex, and if it is too dry, fire is a constant danger.

Rubber is now used for everything from glues and cements to thin latex gloves, foam rubber padding, pipes and valves, shock absorbers, balloons, and diving suits. Three-quarters of the rubber used in the world today is synthetic, made from hydrocarbons.

### IN FOCUS

## Reinventing the Wheel

The first inflatable tire, made of leather and called an aerial wheel, was invented in 1845. Then, in the 1880s, cycling became a craze on both sides of the Atlantic. In 1888 John B. Dunlop, of Belfast, Ireland, patented the first inflatable pneumatic tire for bicycles. This created a huge demand for rubber.

## Check these out:

- Exploitation
- Human Interference
- Plantation
- Tree

Salamanders are amphibians that walk on all fours. They have long bodies, long tails, bulging eyes, and moist, soft skin. Because their skin allows water to escape easily, they can live only in damp places, so the rain forests of Central and South America are ideal habitats for them. They live at every level in the rain forest—under leaves on the forest floor, in forest pools, and even in the canopy in bromeliad (broe-MEE-lee-ad) pools. Salamanders feed on small animals such as insects, worms, and other invertebrates.

## Breathing Without Lungs

Some salamanders have lungs, while others rely on oxygen diffusing through their moist skin and the lining of the mouth. The skin produces slimy mucus that helps to keep it moist and aids oxygen absorption. Tropical salamanders are mostly lungless. They pump their throats to force air into their mouths. Even so, as much as 90 percent of their oxygen is absorbed through the skin itself.

## Courtship and Defense

Some salamanders mate in the water, the male shedding his sperm over the female's eggs as she releases them. The eggs hatch into tiny fishlike larvae, which gradually become more salamander-like as they grow. Other salamanders have a special way of mating. The male produces little packets of sperm, which he places on the ground. Then he guides the female over them until she takes up the sperm packets into her body.

Many tropical salamanders lay their eggs on land in damp places under stones or logs. These eggs are larger and not as numerous as water-laid eggs, since the young will complete their entire development within them, hatching as tiny replicas of their parents. The baby salamanders may take 6 to 12 years to become adults, but they often live for 18 years or more. They shed their skin frequently as they grow.

*A salamander on a leaf in Costa Rica's rain forest. Its webbed feet make it a good swimmer and help it to grip leaves.*

An ideal size of prey for many forest carnivores, several kinds of salamanders produce poisons from glands in their skin and often unpleasant smells, too. Some of these advertise the danger with bright orange or yellow warning colors. Another defense used by a few salamanders is to shed their tail.

## Check these out:
● Amphibian  ● Bromeliad

Scorpions are predatory animals related to spiders. Both groups belong to the class known as arachnids (uh-RAK-nids), though, besides both having eight legs, they have little in common. Scorpions have a more or less oval, flattened body, with huge pincers at the front and a slender, mobile tail at the rear. The tip of the tail carries a poisonous sting. Although they live only in warm places, scorpions are very hardy creatures. They can survive freezing for several weeks. Some scorpions can also survive immersion in water for several hours, and many can go without food for months.

Most of the 650 or so scorpion species live on the ground. They feed mainly at night. Their sight is poor and they tend to ambush their prey rather than go hunting for it. They pick up the vibrations of an approaching victim with slender bristles on their legs and claws. Victims include insects and spiders, along with some lizards and small rodents. The prey is usually caught in the pincers and held firmly while it is torn and crushed by the much smaller jaws. Only the body fluids and the softest tissues are sucked into the scorpion's tiny mouth.

## A Sting in the Tail

Some scorpions use their stings on large prey, especially if it struggles, but the stings are used mainly for defense. To inject its venom, a scorpion curls its tail forward over its body, usually at high speed, and forces the sting into its victim. Small animals are quickly paralyzed or killed. Scorpion stings can be very painful to humans, but only a few scorpions are really dangerous to people—and even these usually sting only if they are disturbed. People are most likely to be stung when they push their hands into crevices where the scorpions are resting.

Several species of scorpions live in the rain forests. The *Pandinus* genus of Africa include some of the world's largest scorpions. Up to 10 inches (25 cm) long, including the claws, they lurk under fallen trunks and branches. Although they can defend themselves against many animals, they do have enemies. Hornbills and some monkeys eat them, but their worst enemies are probably driver ants. Scorpions are not quick enough to get out of the way of the marauding columns of these ferocious insects.

Pandinus imperator *is one of the world's largest scorpions and has extremely large pincers. The jointed tail is folded forward here, and the pale brown bulb of the sting is clearly visible at the tip.*

## Check these out:

- Carnivore
- Invertebrate
- Spider

Seasons and climates are not the same the world over. They depend on where a place is in relation to the equator. Lines of latitude are imaginary circles around the earth. The equator is the line of latitude at 0°. It passes around the middle of the earth, equidistant from the North and South Poles. All the other lines of latitude run parallel to it. The tropics of Cancer and Capricorn are lines of latitiude 23.5° to the north and south of the equator. The area between them, which includes the equatorial area, is known as the Tropics. Generally the Tropics have more light, warmth, and rainfall than the rest of the world, and this is where the world's tropical rain forests are. The areas outside the Tropics have a different, temperate climate. This temperate zone extends to the polar circles, which are 66.5° north and south of the equator.

Spring, summer, autumn, and winter do not exist in the tropical rain forest. Those seasons relate to temperate climates, so they are experienced only in the coastal temperate rain forests, for example in British Columbia, Canada, in the Northern Hemisphere, and in Chile in the Southern Hemisphere. The four seasons are marked by specific weather patterns and begin on set days of the year.

## KEY FACTS

● **Seasonal changes are caused by Earth's movement around the sun.**

● **Tropical rain forests have two seasons—a dry season and a rainy season. Temperate rain forests have four seasons—spring, summer, autumn, and winter.**

● **In Northwestern Brazil between March and August, the Amazon River rises by as much as 50 ft. (15 m).**

*Storm clouds gather at the beginning of Australia's rainy season.*

In North America's temperate rain forest—and in the rest of the Northern Hemisphere—spring begins at the vernal equinox (March 20 or 21) and summer at the summer solstice (June 21 or 22). Autumn begins at the autumnal equinox (September 22 or 23), while winter begins at the winter solstice (December 22 or 23). In the Southern Hemisphere, people have the same seasons, but at different times: summer and winter are reversed, and so are spring and autumn.

*In North America's temperate rain forest there are four seasons. Winter lasts from December to March.*

The reason for these changing seasons is Earth's orbit or path around the sun, which takes one year. Every day of the year, the sun's rays hit the surface of our planet at a slightly different angle. Because Earth is tilted on its axis, for three months of the year the Northern Hemisphere is tilted towards the Sun and experiences summer. Six months later, the Southern Hemisphere is tilted toward the sun. For the other six months, the poles are equidistant from the sun.

**Life in Temperate Rain Forests**

Most of the trees in temperate rain forests are evergreens. In North American rain forests, the main trees are cedar, spruce, and hemlock—tough species that can withstand pelting rain storms. These shelter the few deciduous trees, such as birch, maple, alder, aspen, and willow. The deciduous trees put on a colorful display each autumn, when their leaves gradually change from green to red, purple, brown, orange, or yellow just before they fall. Other temperate rain forests have a different mix of trees: along the Chilean coast, the evergreens are alerce (a type of cypress) and monkey puzzles, which grow alongside deciduous beeches such as Antarctic beech and roble beech.

The wildlife of the temperate rain forests has to be able to adapt to the different seasons. Some animals change their diet, feasting on seeds and berries in autumn and relying on insects or leaves the rest of the year. Animals such as flying squirrels draw on fat reserves during the winter. Many birds simply migrate to the Tropics each autumn and return to nest the next spring when food is plentiful again. Insects cannot survive the cold months, so they lay their eggs in autumn and then die, the eggs hatching the following spring. Salamanders and other amphibians hibernate in the winter, burying themselves beneath the soil. Bears and some other mammals sleep through the winter months, too.

## Tropical Seasons

Things are different near the equator in tropical rain forests, where there are just two seasons—a dry season and a wet season. These seasons, too, are affected by Earth's orbit around the sun. When the sun is at its hottest, directly overhead, storm clouds form and the rains fall. This band of clouds, known as the intertropical convergence zone, shifts from north to south of the equator according to Earth's movement around the sun. Intense heat and heavy rains are nearest the tropic of Cancer in the Northern Hemisphere in June and to the tropic of Capricorn in the Southern Hemisphere in December. At opposite times of the year it is the dry season in each region.

Even during the dry season, at least 4 inches (100 mm) of rain falls each month in tropical rain forests, and it is always hot. The trees here are broad-leaved evergreens. They do not need to shed

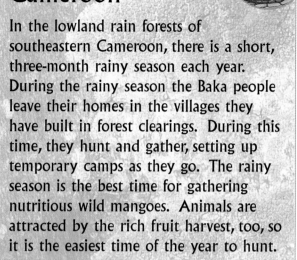

## Seasons in Cameroon

In the lowland rain forests of southeastern Cameroon, there is a short, three-month rainy season each year. During the rainy season the Baka people leave their homes in the villages they have built in forest clearings. During this time, they hunt and gather, setting up temporary camps as they go. The rainy season is the best time for gathering nutritious wild mangoes. Animals are attracted by the rich fruit harvest, too, so it is the easiest time of the year to hunt.

their leaves, because they do not have to survive cold winters. But even though the dry or rainy seasons in these forests might be barely distinguishable, they still have an effect. For example, in the rain forests of Central America, many wild chicle (CHIK-uhl) trees grow. Maya Indians and other people living in the forests collect the chicle's sap, which is a type of latex used to make chewing gum. The sap has to be flowing well inside the tree's trunk for the *chicleros* (chicle-gatherers) to harvest it. This happens during the rainy season, between July and December.

## Subtropical Seasons

Farther from the equator, but still in the Tropics, the dry and rainy seasons become more distinct. In these subtropical forests the average annual rainfall is between 30 and 70 inches (800 and 1,800 mm) a year. Up to three-quarters of the trees might be

*The beginning of the dry season in the Indian monsoon forest. These sambar deer will not roam as far during the dry season, preferring to stick close to rivers and streams, where the grass is lusher and there is enough to drink.*

517

## The Season of Floods

In northwestern Brazil, the wet season brings about a dramatic change. Between March and August, the Amazon rises by as much as 50 ft. (15 m). Only the tallest trees keep their crowns above water—what was the forest floor becomes home to all sorts of fish and mammals, including the rare Amazonian pink dolphin and freshwater manatee. The waters affect the lives of the people who live in the flooded forest. They have to harvest their crops of manioc before the floods come. During the wet season, they navigate the forest floor on long canoes, harpooning or netting the many types of fish, such as pirarucus and tambaqui.

active in the drier months. Other animals, such as monkeys, cats, and lizards, move to parts of the forest that are close to rivers. There, the trees do not lose their leaves, so the food supply remains steady. Some animals adapt by varying their diet. Anteaters eat ants during the wet season and termites during the dry season. Because they are juicier than ants, the termites provide the anteaters with more water.

All these tropical rain forest animals time their breeding seasons so that their young are born when there is a glut of their favorite food. Toucans and macaws, for example, eat fruit and nuts, so they nest during the dry season. Insect-eating birds nest during the wet season, when leaf-eating insects are more active. However, because the climate is always steady, tropical rain forest animals do not change their behavior very much over the year. For example, they do not have to grow thicker fur or hibernate to survive a winter, as animals in temperate rain forests do.

deciduous. Such subtropical rain forests include Southeast Asia's tropical deciduous forests, sometimes called monsoon forests, and Australia's "dry" rain forests. The monsoon forests are made up of deciduous teak trees, as well as thick clumps of bamboo. There are also deciduous rain forests in eastern Brazil and southeastern Africa.

Trees in deciduous rain forests produce their fruit and seeds and shed their leaves at the beginning of the dry season, then sprout new ones when the rains come. Fruit bats and other animals that feast on the trees' dry-season harvest become more

### Check these out:
- Climate and Weather
- Flooding
- Humidity
- Monsoon Rain Forest
- Rain Forest
- Subtropical Rain Forest
- Temperate Rain Forest
- Tropical Rain Forest
- Water

# Seed

Seeds contain the embryos of the next generation of plants. They help spread the forest over new areas of land, and help it regenerate after natural disasters such as hurricanes and volcanic eruptions or after logging. All over the forest, the soil is full of seeds, waiting for space and light to grow.

A seed contains a tiny embryo plant and a store of food provided by the parent plant. The outer coat of the seed, the testa, is very tough, able to resist most attacks by insects and fungi for some time. However, in the moist conditions of the rain forest, it soon softens and the seed germinates: then the tiny embryo root and shoot emerge.

## KEY FACTS

● **The seeds of epiphytic orchids are the smallest in the world.**

● **Some of the largest seeds in the world belong to the coco de mer, the double coconut palm from the Indian Ocean shores, and weigh up to 60 lb. (27 kg).**

● **The rat poison strychnine comes from the seeds of a Southeast Asian plant. Local people use it to tip their arrows and blowpipe darts.**

● **Annatto, often used to color foods such as butter, margarine, and confectionery, comes from the seeds of a tropical American tree.**

## Competition in the Clearings

The seeds of most forest trees are very short-lived: most germinate within a week of reaching the ground. The seeds of pioneer species that colonize newly formed clearings can lie dormant until the right conditions exist. Special chemicals prevent them from germinating until there is sufficient light for the young seedlings to thrive. When one or more giant forest trees fall, perhaps due to a hurricane, lightning, old age, or—more likely—to human saws, these seeds spring to life. Soon the new clearing is full of seedlings of many different kinds, all competing for light, space, and nutrients.

Seeds that germinate on the forest floor need enough food to enable them to put out new roots and leaves until they are big enough to make their own food by photosynthesis. Those sprouting in the shade put all their energies into growing tall and do not expand their leaves until they reach the light.

*A dipterocarp seedling finds a patch of light in which to grow up out of the leaf litter in the Borneo rain forest. The rotting leaves provide it with nutrients. The seedling may grow to be a forest giant.*

## AVOCADO SEED GERMINATION

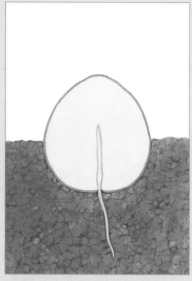

*1. An avocado stone lands on the ground. At its heart is the embryo, which begins to grow.*

*2. The lower half of the embryo is the first to emerge from the seed, and grows down as a single root.*

*3. While the roots develop, the top half of the embryo has emerged as a stalk, and is growing its first leaves.*

Climbing plants such as lianas and Swiss-cheese plants, which may eventually end up high in the canopy, have large seeds with sufficient food reserves to let the young seedlings creep over the forest floor until they find suitable hosts to climb. They may then have a long way to climb before they get enough light for photosynthesis.

### The Need to Travel

Seeds need to be dispersed over a wide area. Conditions near the parent plant may not be suitable for seeds to germinate. The plant itself may be large and the ground below may be heavily shaded. A new sapling would also compete for nutrients with the parent plant. The parent plant may well have grown up in a clearing that no longer exists. Plants will use animals, birds, or the wind to disperse their seeds. Dispersal does risk having seeds land in an unsuitable place, but the tree spreads the risk by producing lots of fruits and seeds.

### Seeds Big and Small

Trees with edible seeds usually produce large numbers of small seeds to spread the risk of their being eaten. Other trees may produce fewer seeds, but these may have poisons in their seed coats that give them a nasty taste. Another tactic is for all the trees of the same species to produce seeds at the same time so that animals cannot possibly eat them all. Large forest trees like mango, durian, and rambutan have seeds that germinate almost immediately, so they do not lie around long enough to get eaten.

Coconut palms have enormous seeds with large food stores, so they can float on the oceans for months or even years before they reach a shore on which to germinate. Some of the smallest seeds in the rain forest are those of rafflesia, a plant that lives as a parasite on vines and has no leaves of its own. Rafflesia seeds are tiny, since they need to carry only enough food for the seedling to reach a suitable host.

*A germinating coconut palm on a tropical beach. Coconuts may drift for thousands of miles across the ocean before coming to rest on a suitable spot.*

## A Fabulous Feast

The fruits produced by rain forest plants to protect and transport their seeds are some of the most important food sources for rain forest animals, from the smallest mouse to the largest bear. In the rain forests of Ghana it has been estimated that 70 percent of all the plant species use animals to disperse their seeds and fruits. The seeds of fleshy fruits usually pass right through the guts of animals and are deposited on the ground with their droppings, often some distance away from the parent tree.

Often plants lure animals with bright colors and strong smells. Many trees produce orange or red fleshy fruits, colors that attract both birds and mammals. Not all the smells are attractive to human noses. The durian of Asia stinks of rotten fish or sewers, and the smell carries for half a mile (0.8 km). The flesh itself does not smell, and both people and animals find it delicious. When a tree is fruiting in the canopy, it can be seen (and smelled) some distance away. To prevent their fruits from being eaten before the seeds are ripe, many fruits have bitter-tasting chemicals in them and advertise this by their green coloring, turning red and sweet when ripe.

## Wind Dispersal

The rain forest is not a windy place. Only the tallest trees in the forest have crowns that stick up above the canopy in the sun and wind. There the air moves at least 100 times faster than down below. But some plants in the understory do use air currents for transport. The tiny, dustlike seeds of orchids are so small that they are easily carried on the lightest of breezes. Silk cotton seeds are covered in silky fluff and drift gently for long distances. Many lianas (lee-AH-nuhs) produce seeds with their own parachutes of hairs.

### IN FOCUS

## Nurse Logs

Where a large tree falls, it creates a gap that allows light to reach the forest floor, so new seedlings can start to grow. The tree itself soon rots. Seeds landing on a rotting log find a moist place with soggy bark and often mossy growths that act like sponges. The seedlings send roots down the side of the log into the rich soil below. As the log continues to rot, it provides more nutrients. Long after the log has vanished and the seedlings have become trees, a line of trees marks the place, often supported on a tunnel of arching stilt roots.

Many of the great forest trees produce seeds or fruits with wings. Possibly the largest of all is *Macrozanonia macrocarpa*, a tropical climber, whose giant winged seed spans 6 inches (15 cm). Another liana, *Alsomitra*, packs several hundred large winged seeds into a pod. When released, they may glide for more than 100 yards (90 m). The winged seeds of some mahogany trees spin as they fall, like little helicopters. This slows their descent, so they travel farther before reaching the ground.

*Young mangrove seedlings sprout from pods while still attached to the parent tree.*

### Floating Seeds

A few plants take advantage of water for dispersal. Probably the best known are the coconut palms that fringe tropical shores. The light fibrous husk that surrounds a coconut allows it to float for months until it washes up on another beach. Seeds of some mangroves living on the fringes of the sea germinate on the parent plant. Then the little plantlets drop into the bare mud below the branch. These plantlets are pointed and spear the soft ground. If they land in water instead, they will float for some distance until they find a patch of ground.

One of the largest seeds of any flowering plant belongs to the Mora trees, tall trees that emerge above the forest canopy. Weighing over 2 pounds (1 kg), these seeds float in the rivers of the Amazon basin, thanks to an air-filled cavity between the leaves of the plant embryo inside the seed. The seeds are very flat, so as soon as they alight on a flat surface, they stay put long enough to germinate.

Not all seeds shed into water need to float. The alligator apple is a fleshy fruit that attracts alligators. The alligators eat the fruits, then pass the seeds out with their droppings. Many trees of seasonally flooded forests, especially those in the Amazon basin, produce fruits that attract fish.

## IN FOCUS

### Hurling Hurus

A few trees provide their own seed propulsion. The huru of tropical South and Central America hurls its seeds explosively up to a distance of 15 yards (14 m). To prevent animals from devouring them, it packs them with a poison so toxic it blisters human skin and can blind if it touches the eyes. Only macaws can eat huru seeds: they devour them before they are ripe, then swallow special clay from the riverbank to deactivate the poisons.

## Check these out:

● Feeding ● Flowering Plant ● Forest Floor ● Light Gap ● Mangrove Forest ● Plant ● Pollination ● Root

Nearly all plants, from the tiniest single-celled alga to the largest tree, need light in order to survive. This is because plants carry out a series of chemical reactions called photosynthesis. During photosynthesis carbon dioxide from the atmosphere and water are used as raw materials to produce sugars. These sugars are the starting point for producing all the other chemicals that make up living things. Photosynthesis takes place in light, and therefore all plants in the wild need to be able to take in at least some light from the sun.

High up in the forest canopy there is plenty of light, but levels fall off very rapidly down through the trees, so very little light reaches the forest floor. Walking through a rain forest is like walking in a gloomy cathedral. The few types of plants that can live on the forest floor are very shade-tolerant and they fall into two main types: ground-dwelling species and slow-growing shrubs and trees.

### KEY FACTS

● As little as one percent of the light that falls on forest trees gets down as far as the forest floor.

● Some shade-tolerant plants cannot stand high levels of light. If a gap appears in the forest when an old tree falls, they die.

### Living in the Dark

Ground-dwelling plants such as ferns carry out their entire life cycle where the light levels are low and the humidity is very high. There is also a small number

*This red-flowered* **Aphelandra** *is a typical plant of deep shade on the rain forest floor. Its ability to tolerate low light makes it an ideal houseplant, so a number of species are cultivated for this purpose.*

# Micro-Forests

Because flowering plants, which live in the semidarkness of the forest floor, grow very slowly, they cannot afford to shed and replace their leaves very often. These leaves are therefore quite long-lived. As a result they become covered in a growth of epiphylls, mosses and other primitive plants that form a tiny forest on the leaf surface. The leaves get even less light and the plant's growth is slowed down further.

of flowering plants that have broad, flat leaves to take in as much light as possible. These include plants such as hot-lips, which can be very abundant in some areas of South and Central American forests, and also some members of the ginger family.

As well as the ground-dwelling species, there are also slow-growing shrubs and trees, which eventually make their way up to higher levels where there is more light and they can grow faster.

**Growing to the Light**
Seeds of some of the main forest trees also germinate and begin to grow in the gloom

of the forest floor. This growth is very slow, much of it depending on food stored up in the seed. What is the advantage of their doing this? Many rain forest tree seeds do not germinate until an old tree falls, leaving a well-lit clearing in the forest into which they can grow. Those that have already germinated in the semidarkness, therefore, have a head start over freshly germinated seeds and can grow very rapidly ahead of them.

**Check these out:**
- Dormancy ● Forest Floor ● Leaf
- Light Gap ● Photosynthesis ● Plant

# Slash and Burn

Slash and burn is a simple and direct way of clearing forest to grow crops. As the name suggests, it consists of cutting down the forest and then setting fire to the fallen trees. It was a very successful system for many thousands of years, and it is still used in some places today. However, the method has some serious drawbacks.

## An Ancient System

Nobody knows how slash-and-burn agriculture began. One theory says that when people first started cutting wood for fires and to build shelters, they noticed that the new, soft growth in the clearings attracted animals they could hunt. Later they planted crops in the clearings, which could supplement the seeds, fruits, and nuts they gathered from the forest. The clearings could be opened up more easily by burning the debris that was too small to be used for firewood.

When a group prepares to slash and burn an area of forest, every able-bodied member of the village goes to the chosen part of the forest and cuts down everything in sight. The piles of wood, branches, and leaves are left to dry in the sun for a few days, and then they are burned. When the ashes cool, they are plowed into the ground and seeds are planted. The ash from the burned trees and shrubs enriches the soil, so that for the first year at least, the crops are good. Later, sometimes even in the second year, the crops fail.

## Failing Crops

There are two main reasons for the failure of crops grown in this way. The first is that the nutrients in the soil are soon used up if the crops are removed without any

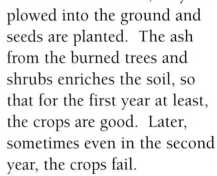

*Slash and burn in Sumatra. The ground is clear and some crops have already been planted, but the trees left standing nearby have also been damaged.*

*Planting crops in newly cleared ground in Madagascar. The almost bare hills behind show that the forest does not grow back properly.*

fertilizer being added. Most rain forests grow on very poor soil and depend on leaves, lichens (LIE-kuhns), and other forest debris to feed the roots of the trees. Without fallen leaves to trap water and rot into the ground, the soil is starved.

The other main reason for crop failure is that animals from the surrounding forest quickly move in, in the form of leaf-eating and sap-sucking insects, plant eaters such as deer, or wild pigs that dig up roots and tubers. When this happens, the village chooses another

## Lost Forests

In Madagascar, slash and burn has caused an ecological disaster. The people who now live in Madagascar came originally from Indonesia, where the forest grew back every time it was left fallow. When they arrived on the huge, ancient island (Madagascar had been isolated for millions of years), they found that this was a different type of forest, which grows back very slowly after it has been burned. As the population grew, more and more forest was destroyed, never to recover. Torrential tropical rain washed the soil away, leaving bare, sterile hills where nothing now will grow.

area of forest and starts again. The first area will recover after about four years, when it can be slashed and burned all over again. This means that a village needs five plots, each big enough to feed all its members, in order to make the system work. Slash and burn supported the Maya people in Mexico for a thousand years. There, too, the wildlife could make use of the four plots that were recovering while the villagers cultivated the fifth. Finally, though, there was not enough land to feed the growing population. The Mayas had to turn to more settled agriculture, but some of their settlements collapsed from lack of food-growing space close enough to their cities.

## Check these out:
● Cattle Ranching  ● Clear-Cutting
● Deforestation  ● Erosion  ● Human
Interference  ● Madagascar

526

# Sloth

Sloths are extraordinary animals. Though they are among the most common mammals in the rain forests of Central and South America, they are seldom seen. Camouflaged in the canopy by their shaggy yellow or brownish fur, they spend all their time either eating or sleeping. Active for only 7 to 8 hours a day, they survive on their nutrient-poor diet of leaves by moving very slowly, reducing their energy requirement. A sloth may travel only 130 feet (40 m) in a whole day. Their body temperature fluctuates more than most mammals, so they use less energy keeping warm. Like cold-blooded animals, they bask in the sun to warm up and move into the shade to cool down.

There are five species of sloths, two species of two-toed sloths and three species of three-toed sloths. Actually all sloths have three toes, but the two-toed ones have only two claws. Most sloths eat a variety of leaves and stems and sometimes fruits. A sloth takes a long time to process the tough leaves it eats: the food in its stomach and intestines may make up 30 percent of its entire body weight.

A sloth spends most of its life upside down. It hangs below the branches of trees by its paws, which have large curved claws like grappling hooks. About once a week the sloth descends to the ground to urinate and pass its droppings, usually in a favorite place, perhaps to advertise its presence to other sloths or even to suitors. Then it slowly climbs back up a tree. Sloths are also surprisingly good swimmers.

Sloths have only one young at a time. The female gives birth while hanging in the tree, and the baby grows up in a living hammock. The young sloth stays with its mother for up to nine months and is fully grown at about three years of age. Sloths may live for about 20 years.

*A sloth spends almost its entire life upside down. Predators walking along its branch may fail to notice it. The muscles in its feet rest in a gripping state, even when the animal is dead.*

## Check these out:
- Canopy
- Central America
- Herbivore
- Mammal
- Symbiosis

Slugs and snails look very different at first sight—snails have coiled shells and most slugs have no shells at all—but the animals are closely related. Slugs are really just snails that have lost their shells during their evolution. They all belong to a group of mollusks called gastropods. This name means "belly foot" and refers to the fact that the animals appear to glide around on their bellies, although the muscular part on which they glide is actually called the foot.

## KEY FACTS

● Land-living slugs and most land-living snails have eyes at the tips of their tentacles, but their eyesight is not very good. They withdraw their tentacles when they bump into things.

● Slugs and most land-living snails are hermaphrodites. This means that each animal has both male and female parts. They still need to mate, but each one can then lay eggs.

● The shells of some giant African snails can be up to 8 in. (20 cm) long.

A normal snail's shell is made largely of calcium, with a horny layer on the outside that provides most of the color. Many rain forest soils are deficient in calcium, so snails living in the rain forest generally have very thin shells. Some of the shells consist entirely of the horny material, with no calcium at all. The shell is secreted by a thick cloak of skin called the mantle, which covers much of the snail's body. Although most slugs have lost their shells, they still retain the mantle, which usually covers the front half of the body.

## Herbivores and Carnivores

Thousands of species of slugs and snails live on the rain forest floor, where fungi (FUN-jie) and fallen leaves provide abundant food throughout the year. Lots of tiny snails flourish in the debris trapped around the bases of epiphytic plants. Some species, including Africa's giant snails, attack living plants, and there are also many carnivorous snails in the rain forests. They all feed with the aid of a horny tongue called a radula. This is covered with thousands of minute teeth that shred the food like a cheese grater.

## Africa's Giants

The world's largest land snails live in Africa. The largest species (*Achatina*

*These courting slugs in a Kenyan rain forest could easily be mistaken for dead and shriveled leaves.*

*fulica*) originated in East Africa, outside the rain forests, but it has been transported—accidentally or purposefully—to many other areas. It has now established itself in many forested areas of Southeast Asia, where it causes serious damage to all sorts of crops. Despite its size, this giant's brown-and-orange shell is quite well camouflaged among the dead leaves on the ground.

Several species of *Achatina* live around the edges of the rain forests, wherever the soil can supply sufficient calcium for their shells. Some of these shells reach 8 inches (20 cm) in length, and a complete snail can weigh over 8 ounces (230 g). In parts of West Africa these giant snails are a major source of protein for the people.

**Rain Forest Slugs**

Most rain forest slugs resemble those living elsewhere. Because they have no shells, they are not dependent on calcium and can live in a wider range of habitats than the snails. Like the snails, they include carnivorous and herbivorous species, although most species feed on

*The two pairs of tentacles, with the eyes at the tips of the longer ones, are clearly visible in this ground–living rain forest snail.*

rotting vegetation. *Veronicella* species and their relatives are unusual in having a mantle that extends all across the body. Their tentacles contract like accordians instead of being pulled in like the tentacles of most other slugs.

## IN FOCUS

### Endangered Snails

Most rain forest snails are quite drab, but some have colorful shells. *Papustyla* species are tree-living snails in the forests of New Guinea. Their brilliant yellow-and-green shells were once used to make jewelry. The snails have now become rare and trading in them is banned by CITES—the Convention on International Trade in Endangered Species of Wild Fauna and Flora.

## Check these out:
- Carnivore  ● Decomposer  ● Herbivore
- Invertebrate

# Snake

Snakes are long, thin reptiles without any legs. They are cold-blooded, meaning that their bodies cannot regulate their temperature when it gets cold or hot, so they are active only when the temperature around them is warm. The smallest tropical snakes are about 5 inches (12 cm) long, while the largest are over 30 feet (9 m) long.

Snakes are silent predators that glide up to their prey or lie in wait for it. Some hunt on the forest floor, their brown, yellow, and black patterns blending with the dead leaves and dappled sunlight. They can slide under logs and into crevices in search of prey, and some even burrow into the soil. Other snakes hunt in the trees.

## Designed to Kill

Most snakes seize their prey in their jaws. They have formidable needle-sharp teeth, or fangs, that usually point backward to prevent the prey from escaping. Vipers, which have particularly long fangs, keep them folded back when not in use, swinging them into action as they strike at their prey.

The bushmasters of South America are aggressive animals and highly territorial. A bushmaster will even chase humans who venture into its patch. Another fearsome snake is the jumping viper of Central America. It leaps into the air to strike down on its victims.

While some snakes actively pursue their prey, others rely on ambush. Vine snakes, found throughout the Tropics, grow up to 5 feet (1.5 m) long, yet they are so thin and light that they can wrap their tail around a branch and extend over half their body into the air to reach the next branch. Some can even hold themselves rigid in midair so that they resemble vines as they lie in wait for passing birds.

*A parrot snake opens its mouth wide to reveal the bright pink interior in a threat display.*

Pythons and boa constrictors crush their prey to death. Coiling their powerful bodies around the prey, they exert a deadly pressure. Every time the prey breathes out, the python tightens its coils, so each breath is shallower than the last. Some of the larger pythons, such as the African python and the reticulated and Indian pythons of Asia, can take prey as large as goats and pigs. The mussurana of tropical America combines techniques: it uses venom to kill smaller prey such as mice and constriction to kill other snakes.

Snakes swallow their prey whole. Their teeth are adapted for gripping and killing, not for chewing or cutting up food. They have amazing elasticated jaws. These jaws can dislocate: they are held together only by elastic tissue. This gives the snake a huge gape. With its backward-pointing fangs, the snake walks its jaws over its prey, pushing it down its throat. The skin between its scales can stretch to accommodate a large meal.

**Injecting Poison**

Snakes are famous for their venom, but not all snakes are venomous, and danger is not always related to size. A bite from a baby fer-de-lance from Central and South America can knock out a grown man. Many poisonous snakes produce their venom at the base of the fangs, which have grooves for channeling the poison.

Snake venoms work in a variety of ways. Cobra venom is a nerve poison, causing breathing difficulties, heart problems, and often paralysis. Some cobras spit in the eyes of their attackers. The venom can accurately strike a victim 7 feet (2 m) away and may cause temporary or even permanent blindness. Viper venom is not as potent, but there is more of it. It acts mainly on the blood and muscles, causing pain, swelling, bruising, and other very unpleasant symptoms.

**IN FOCUS**

## Blind Snakes

There are many burrowing snakes that feed on earthworms or ants and termites. Many have strong, broad heads with pointed snouts and small eyes, finding their prey by touch, smell, and vibrations. The blind snakes found in most parts of the Tropics carry these adaptations to an extreme. They have only traces of eyes hidden under the scales on the head. Blind thread snakes of Africa and tropical America are extremely slender. Some lay their eggs in the safety of termite nests, where the termite larvae will serve as food for the snake's young.

## Camouflage and Other Defenses

For most snakes the first line of defense is camouflage: the ability to blend into the background. Camouflage conceals a snake from both its enemies and its prey. The bold patterns on snakes such as the reticulated python and the bushmaster disguise the shape of the coils as the snakes lie in wait on the forest floor. Fast-moving snakes are often striped: the stripes run the length of their bodies and disguise the effect of motion. The emerald tree boa of South America and the green tree snakes of South America and Australia look gaudy, but they are well camouflaged for their life in the canopy.

Bright colors can have other advantages. The African vine snake uses its yellow or red tongue as a lure to draw prey closer as they mistake it for a worm. If threatened, pipe snakes of South America and Asia will hide their heads and wiggle their tails, which have head-like markings and a red underside. This diverts a predator's attention to the least vulnerable part of the snake's body.

The coral snakes of the Americas have poisonous flesh or venomous bites and

# Making Antivenin

Antidotes to specific snake venoms are made by immunizing horses or other animals with a weakened version of the venom that will not harm them, milked from snakes that have been farmed for the purpose. The immunized animals develop antibodies (immune system chemicals) that will attack the venom if they encounter it again. These antivenins can be injected into humans who have been bitten.

advertise the fact with bright red, orange, or yellow-and-black stripes. This is really to deter predators from attacking them. However, some snakes cheat: if they live in a region where such poisonous snakes are common, they evolve a similar coloration. Thus they gain protection without the cost of producing the poison. Such mimicry works only if the mimics are less common than the subject. For warning colors to work, predators must be able to learn from experience. Such colors are not necessary if a snake's venom is lethal, as no animal would learn from the experience of tackling one.

There are other kinds of deception. Many cobras have eyelike markings on the back of the hood to deceive any predators that approach from behind.

*A green vine snake lies in wait for passing birds or other animals, holding its body rigid to mimic a vine.*

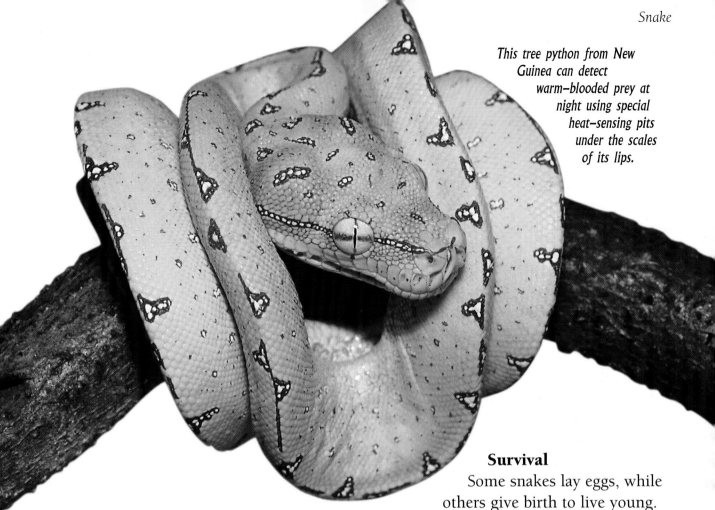

*This tree python from New Guinea can detect warm–blooded prey at night using special heat–sensing pits under the scales of its lips.*

## Locomotion

At first sight it is hard to imagine how an animal with no legs can move over the ground, especially a large, heavy snake like a python.  The snake throws its body into a series of curves, which push against small bumps in the ground, stones, or rough patches of bark, propelling the snake forward.  Tree snakes climb trees by pushing their coils sideways against ridges in the bark. Some vipers travel in almost a straight line by using their scales in a similar way: muscles attached to each scale can raise or lower it.

Some snakes are good swimmers, but only a few snakes have taken to the air. The flying snakes of Asia are slender tree snakes.  A flying snake will launch itself from a branch, then straighten its body and pull in its belly to form a concave ribbon, an ideal shape for gliding.

## Survival

Some snakes lay eggs, while others give birth to live young. Egg-laying females may stay to guard their eggs.  The king cobra from Asia lays up to 40 eggs in a nest of leaves and guards them fiercely.  The Indian python actually warms her eggs by coiling around them and shivering: the active muscles generate heat.

While some snakes can kill people, they usually do so only when they are being milked for their venom, exhibited, or otherwise disturbed.  As the human population continues to expand, encounters between people and snakes happen more and more often.  Hunted for their attractive skins, medicines, charms, and the pet trade, many snakes today are in serious decline.

## Check these out:
- Camouflage
- Carnivore
- Cobra
- Constrictor
- Locomotion
- Reptile

Although South America is only the fourth largest continent, it is still almost twice the size of Europe. The two-thirds of South America's area that lie within the Tropics contain the world's largest rain forest, occupying most of the area known as Amazonia. South America has by far the largest area of rain forest of any continent.

Amazingly enough, the westernmost regions of the lush Amazonian forests, reaching far up the slopes of the Andes mountains, are only narrowly separated from cactus-filled deserts that occupy the mountain slopes facing the Pacific Ocean. This desert becomes drier and more barren as you head downward, so that by the time you reach the coast, life may be completely absent from many areas. If you fly inland from the coast, a line of demarcation is clearly visible as you fly across the crest of the Andes—brown and dry on one side, green and lush on the other. This is a dramatic illustration of the effects of what is known as rain shadow, in this case caused by the towering peaks of the Andes.

Moisture-laden winds sweeping westward off the Atlantic Ocean drop much of their rain on the leafy Amazonian forests. These then regenerate much of the rain as cloud, which is redistributed over the forest as yet more rain. As the clouds reach the lower slopes of the Andes, they rise and begin to cool. Because cool air cannot hold as much water as warm air, the clouds are forced to release most of their water as rain. By the time the clouds reach the top of the Andes, they have been wrung almost dry and only occasionally manage to make their way over the top and drop life-giving rain on the desert on the other side. Cool coastal currents in the Pacific Ocean prevent any rain from arriving over the desert from that direction. There is hardly a better example of the dramatic effects of rainfall on biodiversity than this forest and desert existing side by side. On one side is the Amazonian rain forest, with its thousands of species of trees and million or so species of animals; on the other,

### KEY FACTS

● **South America covers about 13 percent of the world's land surface.**

● **The Chocó rain forests of Colombia receive a staggering 500 in. (12,700 mm) of rain a year.**

● **Colombia contains just under one-fifth of all the world's bird species.**

● **South America has the world's only nocturnal monkey—the night or owl monkey.**

● **Much rain forest has been cut down to grow coca plants to produce cocaine.**

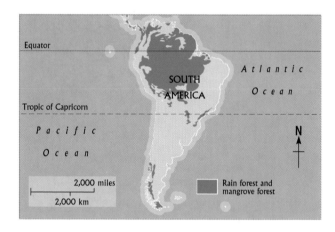

Equator

SOUTH AMERICA

Atlantic Ocean

Tropic of Capricorn

Pacific Ocean

N

2,000 miles
2,000 km

Rain forest and mangrove forest

the Atacama Desert of Chile and the Sechura Desert of Peru, in which many areas have a biodiversity count of zero.

As well as the huge Amazonian rain forest, which sprawls like a giant green inkblot across the heart of the continent, South America also contains some other smaller areas of rain forest. Up in the northwest there is a belt of very species-rich forest running down the western side of Ecuador and Colombia; there the Chocó region receives some of the highest rainfall on Earth.

To the south lie subtropical rain forests stretching down to the borders of Brazil, Paraguay, and Argentina, around the great waterfalls of Iguaçu. Temperate rain forest still thrives near the coast in southern Chile.

## Biodiversity

South America holds two of the world's so-called megadiversity countries—Colombia and Brazil. Colombia is one of the world's richest nations on an inch-for-inch comparison of the number of species it contains. Although it

*This waterfall in Ecuador's Cayambe–Coca Ecological Reserve is surrounded by lush rain forest filled with an amazing diversity of plants and animals.*

535

## Brazil's Atlantic Coast

Rain forest used to extend in a broad belt along the Atlantic coast of Brazil. This forest once covered about 12 percent of the country, but most of it has now been destroyed and replaced with poor-quality pastureland, often on steep slopes subject to damaging erosion. The numerous kinds of plants and animals unique to these forests are now tottering on the brink of extinction in the 2 percent that still remains, mostly in quite small parcels. Fortunately some of the biggest and best examples are protected as reserves, which contain some of the world's most endangered animals, such as the muriqui (a monkey), golden lion tamarin, and buffy-headed marmoset.

occupies less than one percent of the world's land area, it holds more than 10 percent of the world's plants and animals, and the known total is constantly growing. It can boast a total of 50,000 species of higher plants (ferns, club mosses, conifers, and flowering plants, not including liverworts and mosses), a truly amazing number when compared with the mere 30,000 species found in the whole massive area of Africa south of the Sahara. Colombia also leads the world in orchid species—about 3,500—which is also more than all of Africa, and holds the top spot for birds, with about 1,720 species. In fact, if mammals, amphibians, and reptiles were added to this total, thereby including all the terrestrial vertebrates, Colombia comes number three in the world, with around 3,000 species. Of course, not all this fantastic array of biodiversity is restricted to Colombia's rain forests, as it also has high mountain and semidesert habitats, but the rain forests hold the bulk of the species. The Colombian rain forests are also home to many peoples who still practice their traditional customs and have a great deal of priceless knowledge about the medicinal value of rain forest plants.

South America shares most of its rain forest plant and animal families with Central America, via the narrow neck of land connecting the continents of North and South America. Taken by itself, South America is by far the richest of the continents in terms of many kinds of creatures, such as birds and butterflies. A single small area of Amazonia may be home to more kinds of butterflies than occur in all of Africa or in any of the main regions of Asia. South America is also unusual in having many different species of small day-active primates—the tamarins and marmosets, with no comparable examples even in Central America, let alone Africa or Asia.

In Africa there are many small forest antelopes that graze within the shady forest understory, comparable to the several kinds of deer that do the same thing in Asia, but in South America their place is taken by large rodents, such as the agouti, the paca, and the capybara, the world's largest rodent. The agouti is particularly important for distributing seeds around the forest, as fallen fruits are its main source of food. Although it eagerly devours the whole fruit during times of scarcity, in times of plenty it buries a proportion for later consumption, but it often forgets where it has put them, thereby helping in seed dispersal. The pig-sized capybara (from a South American Indian word meaning "master of the grasses") is found widely in the forests but is most common along the Amazon and other rivers, where large family groups may be seen trotting along like pigs. It is common on the huge floating meadows alongside the Amazon, swimming well with its partially webbed feet, while its nostrils are set high on the nose, keeping them clear of the water.

## South American Rain Forest Reserves

South America probably leads the world in the number of rain forest reserves that have been privately purchased in order to conserve their habitat and its unique plants and animals. These reserves range from small patches of a few hundred acres, to massive areas covering thousands of acres of pristine forest. As a top priority

most of these reserves have quickly established good facilities for tourists. Expert biologists are often on hand to lead the first-time visitor into the forest and reveal its secrets via extensive networks of paths. Ecuador has by far the largest number of these reserves, such as the Jatun Sacha Biological Station in Amazonia. This is dedicated to research into the rain forest and its conservation and to education for the public about the forest environment. The reserve is rich in wildlife, including some 68 amphibian, 358 bird, and 750 butterfly species. (Some South American reserves, such as Rancho

*Pale green tree ferns gleam in the dense understory of Brazil's Intervales State Park in São Paulo. This part of the highly endangered Atlantic rain forest contains some of South America's rarest animals.*

Grande in Brazil, have over 1,500 species of butterflies.)

Many rain forest lodges and reserves make every effort to minimize their impact on the environment, with close attention to disposal of wastes, while electricity is produced by solar power. At Kapawi Lodge and Ecological Reserve in Ecuador, the main effort is to preserve the forest for the benefit of the local Achuar Indian people while also allowing outsiders to view the forest and its inhabitants, both animals and human. The easiest large animals to see in all these reserves are monkeys, which rapidly become tame once they are no longer hunted and get used to seeing humans every day.

## Rain Forest Destruction

The destruction of South America's rain forest is of huge concern to environmentalists. Large areas of forest in the Amazon basin have disappeared under water as dams have been built to provide huge reservoirs for the generation of electricity. Other areas have been cleared by logging companies, by cattle ranchers, and by mining companies. As a result of increasing human populations and their need for food, much of the forest is still being cut down, burned, and then used for short-term crop production. If this rate of destruction continues, there will be little rain forest left in South America by the middle of the 21st century.

## IN FOCUS

# The Toucan

South America is very much a continent of birds, with about one-third of the world's species. In Amazonia alone live a staggering 10 percent of all the world's birds; just under half of these are not found anywhere else. Among the most conspicuous of South American birds are the toucans, with their large and colorful beaks. Toucans eat mainly fleshy fruits, sometimes cracking a hard outer case with their powerful beak to get at the soft insides.

## Check these out:

- Amazonia
- Biodiversity
- Bird
- Central America
- Deforestation
- Hydroelectricity
- National Park
- Rain Forest
- Rodent
- Toucan
- Tourism

# Spider

Spiders are commonly confused with insects, but spiders have eight legs and insects have only six. Most adult insects also have wings but spiders never have wings. More than 35,000 different species of spiders have been described. The animals occur in just about every terrestrial habitat, but, like most other cold-blooded animals, the greatest number of species live in the Tropics. This is also where the largest spiders live.

## Hunting and Killing Prey

Spiders are all predatory creatures. Most of them feed on insects, and many spin elaborate silken webs for trapping prey. The best known of these webs are the wheel-shaped orb webs, which are spun in all kinds of vegetation as well as on fences and buildings. The circular threads are sticky, and flying insects that bump into the webs are securely trapped. Other familiar webs include the more or less flat hammock and sheet webs. These are not sticky, but insects walking or falling onto them find their feet trapped in the dense mesh of silk threads. Many spiders make no webs at all. These include the hunters that stalk or chase their prey and the ambushers that merely lie in wait for something to arrive.

All but a few small spiders kill or paralyze their prey with venom. This is injected into the prey through the fangs

## KEY FACTS

● Some spiders can sit comfortably on a pinhead, but the biggest ones have legs that would stretch all the way across a dinner plate.

● The biggest spider fangs belong to the Goliath tarantula. They are about half an inch (13 mm) long and they are used like pickaxes to dig the spider's burrows and for stabbing its prey.

● Most spiders have poor eyesight, despite having six or eight eyes.

● Tiny spiders of the genus *Curimagua* live on the heads of large tarantulas and steal some of their food, but they are so small that the tarantulas take no notice of them.

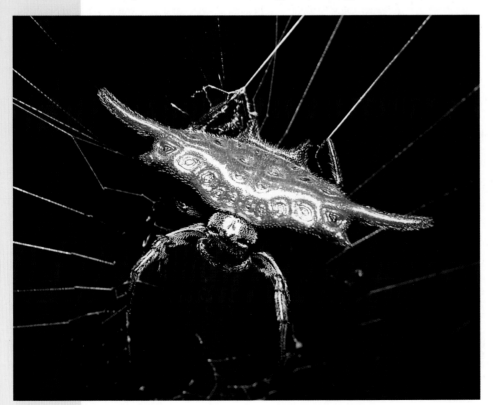

*A bird would find this red kite spider very hard to swallow because of the spines on its body.*

when the spiders bite. Many orb web spiders wrap their victims in silk, either before or after biting them. As well as immobilizing the victim, the venom breaks down or digests the soft tissues so that the spider can suck them up. Some spider venoms are extremely poisonous, but only about 30 species produce enough venom to be dangerous to people. Most spider fangs are unable to pierce human skin.

## IN FOCUS

## Spider Silk

Although not all spiders make webs like the golden orb weaver below, they all make silk. In fact, they make several kinds of silk, and each kind has a particular purpose. One or more kinds may be used for building a web, while another is used for wrapping the prey, and another is used for protecting the eggs. Each kind of silk is produced in a gland in the spider's abdomen and is drawn out through microscopic pores on the spinnerets at the rear of the body. A silk strand emerging from a single pore may be less than one millionth of an inch thick, but lots of strands stick together to form the threads that we see. These threads are the strongest of all natural fibers—even stronger than steel wires of the same thickness. They are also very elastic. Some spider silk can be stretched to several times its original length before it breaks.

## Orb Web Spiders

The biggest orb webs are made by various species of *Nephila*, which occur in all tropical forests. The females of some of these spiders have leg spans of about 6 inches (15 cm), and their webs are often more than a yard (1 m) in diameter. They are slung between the trees and, as well as catching butterflies and moths, they often trap small birds. Even people walking into large webs may be stopped in their tracks. The indigenous people living in the rain forests of Southeast Asia sometimes gather the webs on frameworks of twigs and use them as fishing nets.

Many smaller orb webs are slung in the rain forest canopy. There are plenty of insects there for the spiders to feed on, but also plenty of birds and lizards that like to feed on the spiders. Several of the orb web spiders living here, including various species of *Gasteracantha*, are protected by spiny outgrowths on their abdomens. Predators would find it difficult and probably quite painful to swallow one of these spiders, but the spiders generally have bright colors that warn predators to keep well away from them.

## Fishing for Moths

Several species of bolas spiders live in the rain forests. Each evening the spider spins a single strand of silk, up to two inches (5 cm) long, with one or more blobs of glue on the end, and then whirls the thread around with one of its legs. At the same time the spider gives out a scent just like that of certain female moths. The male moths find it irresistible, and they fly toward the spider. It is not long before one is trapped by a whirling blob of glue.

## Big Bird Eaters

The world's biggest spiders live in the rain forests. Largest of all is the Goliath tarantula of Amazonia. This hairy monster has a body about 3½ inches (8 cm) long and a leg span of about 10 inches (25 cm).

*The radiating tripwires are clearly seen around the lair of this giant trap-door spider from Malaysia.*

Hiding in a deep burrow by day, it comes out to hunt on the forest floor at night. Frogs, lizards, and small rodents make up most of its food. The Goliath and its relatives are often called bird-eating spiders because they sometimes catch roosting birds and take hatchlings from their nests. The big fangs of the tarantulas lie side by side and are plunged into the prey like two daggers. The fangs of most other spiders come together like tongs when the spider bites.

Tarantulas are not really dangerous to people. Their bites are painful, but their barbed hairs are more of a problem because they can work their way into the skin and cause severe irritation.

Spider

## Hidden Trapdoors

Several spiders live in silk-lined burrows fitted with hinged lids or doors. The spiders camouflage their doors with debris from their surroundings, and it is very difficult to see them. When it is hungry, the spider opens the door a fraction and sits underneath it, sometimes with its front legs just poking out. As soon as anything comes by, the spider darts out and catches it and then retires to its burrow to enjoy its meal. The various *Liphistius* species living in Southeast Asia are commonly called giant trap-door spiders because some have bodies up to two inches (5 cm) long. Each one fixes eight radiating threads to its trapdoor, so it receives an early indication of any prey moving in the vicinity of its burrow.

## Jumping Jewels

Jumping spiders are often called jumping jewels. Many of them have brilliantly colored and often iridescent hairs. With over 4,000 species, they form the largest of all spider families. Most of them live in the Tropics, and this is certainly where the most colorful ones occur.

Males are especially colorful, and they show off their colors to the females during spectacular courtship dances.

Rarely more than half an inch (1 cm) long, many of these spiders hunt on tree trunks. Having spotted its prey from a distance, the spider creeps to within an inch or two (2.5 to 5 cm) of it. Then it jumps—but not before anchoring a silken lifeline securely to the bark in case it falls. The prey is pinned down with the stout front legs, and then the fangs get to work. Big eyes staring out from the front of the head give the jumping spider superb eyesight. The eyes work like simple telescopes and allow the spider to focus clearly on its prey. These eyes are actually larger than the spider's brain.

*Orsima ichneumon* from Southeast Asia is a tiny green, red, and black spider. It is one of the strangest of the jumping spiders and actually looks more like an insect. The shiny black tip of its abdomen is swollen and, with two slender spinnerets resembling feelers, it looks just like an insect's head. Birds mistaking this for the head of a true insect get a surprise when the spider leaps away in the opposite direction. Many other spiders and insects deceive their enemies with similar back-to-front camouflage.

## Crab Spiders

Crab spiders have squat bodies. With their first two pairs of legs much larger than the others, they look like small crabs. They usually lie in wait for prey and grab anything of the right size that comes within range of their front legs.

*The seven-spined crab spider from Brazil is easily mistaken for a part of the flower. Insects that make this mistake pay for it with their lives.*

Crab spiders sit on bark, leaves, or flowers and are usually very well camouflaged, so their victims do not see them until it is too late. Some can even change color to some extent to match

*The Goliath tarantula, the world's biggest spider, regularly catches small mammals as well as insects. This one has caught a mouse.*

different backgrounds. The seven-spined crab spider from the rain forests of South America looks just like a small white flower, but insects that land on it soon discover their mistake.

Male spiders are usually much smaller than the females, and mating can be a dangerous business. If the males do not give the right signals, they are likely to be eaten. The males of many web-spinning species play tunes on the females' webs by plucking the threads in a way that the females recognize. Wolf spiders and jumping spiders signal to the females by waving their palps or front legs.

## IN FOCUS

## The Gladiator Spider

Several kinds of gladiator spider live in the rain forests. They throw their webs over their prey, in much the same way that the ancient gladiators used to snare each other. These twiglike spiders hang upside-down close to the ground, and hold a small rectangular web in their front legs. When an insect comes into range, the spider lunges forward, stretches its web, and drops it over the victim. Gladiators feed at night and spot approaching prey with two huge eyes. These eyes give them a fierce appearance, which explains why they are sometimes called ogre-faced spiders.

## Check these out:
● Camouflage ● Insectivore ● Invertebrate
● Nocturnal Animal

# Glossary

**Ambush**: to lie in wait for prey, usually well concealed, and then take it by surprise when it comes within reach.

**Aquatic**: living in or on the water of oceans, ponds, lakes, streams, or rivers.

**Beds**: prepared areas of soil used for sowing seeds or planting seedlings or cuttings.

**Biodiversity**: biological diversity; the variety of plant and animal species in a given area.

**Camouflage**: a form of deception, particularly one involving the use of concealing colors and patterns, that enables an animal to avoid the attention of its enemies or its prey.

**Carbon dioxide**: an invisible gas present in Earth's atmosphere and forming part of the air pollution given out by factories and traffic. It is absorbed by green plants.

**Carnivorous**: feeding on the flesh of animals.

**Deciduous**: describes trees that shed their leaves each year.

**Dengue fever**: a tropical disease that causes terrible fevers and a rash but is seldom fatal.

**Dry rain forest**: a type of subtropical rain forest found in sheltered areas in which there is 24–43 inches (600–1,100 mm) of rainfall a year and a marked dry season.

**Economics**: the way in which labor, goods, and money are used and managed in society.

**Ecosystem**: the natural balance of plants and animals that live within a particular environment and depend upon one another for their survival.

**Enclave**: a small pocket of a particular type of territory that is surrounded by a different type of territory.

**Fang**: a spider's jaw or one of the enlarged teeth of a snake that are used to inject venom into prey.

**Germination**: the beginning of growth of a seed to form a new plant.

**Hemisphere**: half of the globe or world.

**Herbivorous**: feeding entirely on plants or vegetable matter.

**Humidity**: a measure of the amount of water vapor held by the atmosphere.

**Indigenous**: belonging originally to a place.

**Influenza**: a very contagious disease caused by a virus. Its symptoms include headaches, fever, aching joints, and breathing difficulties.

**Lassa fever**: a highly-lethal viral disease.

**Latex**: the white, sticky sap of a rubber tree.

**Malaria**: a disease that causes terrible fevers and sometimes death. It is transmitted by a parasite carried by mosquitoes and enters a person's bloodstream through mosquito bites.

**Mollusk**: any member of the large group of invertebrate animals that includes cockles, slugs, and snails. They all have soft bodies that are generally enclosed in a protective shell.

**Oxbow lakes**: curved lakes that were once part of but no longer joined to a river, left behind after the river has moved from its original course.

**Palpus** (*pl. palps*): a pair of appendages that are sensitive to touch and taste. Spiders use them the same way that insects use their antennae.

**Photosynthesis**: the process by which green plants combine water and carbon dioxide from the air to make simple sugars, which they use as energy-giving food.

**Pneumatic**: inflated with air.

**Predatory**: describes animals that catch and eat other animals.

**Propagation**: the reproduction of plants either as a natural process or by sowing seeds or taking cuttings.

**Spinneret**: any of the slender appendages at the rear of a spider's body through which the silk emerges. Most spiders have six spinnerets.

**Subtropical**: describes areas with a tropical climate and habitat but that lie just outside the Tropics, i.e., north of the Tropic of Cancer and south of the Tropic of Capricorn.

**Temperate rain forest**: forests with high rainfall in the temperate regions of the world that have a distinct winter and summer.

**Topsoil**: the upper layers and surface of the soil, in which plants take root.

**Tributaries**: small streams or rivers that flow into larger streams or rivers.

**Venom**: a poison that is injected into another animal in some way—usually through fangs or stings. It may be used for defense or to kill or paralyze prey.

**Vertebrate**: any animal that possesses a backbone, e.g., fish, amphibians, reptiles, birds, and mammals.

# Index

All numbers in *italics* indicate photographs.